CHAPTER 1
INTRODUCTION

Never before in our country's history has the cost of Shelter been so high. Despite centuries of Empire, Industrial Progress and high Wealth, in the 21st century the cost of housing is the highest it has ever been, relative to our wages, to the point that it feels like there has been no progress over the last 1,000 years where affordability is concerned. Despite having the greatest Empire the world ever saw and the benefits it brought, and despite being the epicentre of the Industrial Revolution, there has been very little progress. Why is it that despite all this progress over several hundred years, our younger generation cannot afford the cost of basic Shelter?

It is interesting how views of unaffordability over house prices have changed over the past 10 years. Whereas before it was mainly younger people who were concerned about affording a house, this view has now spread to much broader sections of society as a whole. Parents are concerned that they cannot afford to upsize. Middle aged people realise that they would not be able to afford to buy again if they needed to at today's wages. Older people with grown-up children are concerned how their children and grandchildren are going to afford basic things in life, which they themselves were able to do.

For those Millennials who have given up trying to understand why the housing market is in the state that it is, why you cannot afford to buy, This Book is for You. For those Parents who want their children to have the same opportunities for homeownership in this country, This Book is for You. For those few people in the political sphere who truly want to reform Land and Property law in the UK, This Book is also for You. The mainstream Politicians out there would do well to read this, as solving the long-term housing crisis in this country is arguably within the top 3 most important issues this country faces.

For those of the over-40s, the so-called Generation-Xers and Baby-Boomers, you are still economically productive in our society. By and large most of you managed to get onto the housing ladder when prices were still affordable, and so you are probably satisfied with the house you are living in. But I urge you to be open-minded when reading this book as to the effect that the housing market since the 2nd world war has had on your ability to realise *your* dreams, perhaps of upsizing or building your own home, where you want to - and the future for your descendants.

My own experience of the housing market in this country has been frustrating to the point that I have all but given up. I would like to renovate or rebuild a property. It always seems to be a Seller's market, and they just seem to be able to get away with charging a lot of money for what is arguably poor quality houses and Land.

I have seen for too many years the way the Establishment Elite have only half-heartedly talked about the housing market, because the issue does not affect them personally. I have seen how insensitive most of their comments have been, and yes, in some cases downright provocative. Yes, the housing crisis gets talked about and everybody knows it is out there, but the real truth and hard-hitting facts about why it is here, funnily enough, do not get mentioned on the media in anything like the depth that is needed. So here is my response.

I want to show you that in this book, the reason that you cannot afford to buy a house, or would not afford to buy if you were buying again for the first time, is because a whole selection of laws have been enacted that have effectively Rigged the Housing Market in favour of ever-higher prices. I aim to show you that it may been deliberately Rigged. Politicians and commentators can talk about how the housing market has 'structural issues' causing the high prices. But there is a much bigger picture than that, and quite frankly 'structural issues' sounds at best like a metaphor, a misnomer, and an excuse for something much worse.

This book aims to show you how a succession of Laws instigated by successive Labour and Conservative governments over the course of 70 years of post-war history have accumulated to essentially Rig the Housing Market in this country towards ever-higher prices, especially relative to our Wages. Nowhere else in the world has this been done to this extent. And nowhere else in the world has it enabled the Establishment Elite and Immoral People to make so much money in a relatively short space of time. All too often it seems that being 'in Property' is the business of all too many suspect characters, immoral people and outright criminals. Property is a classic way for criminals and corrupt public figures to launder money and use their position to make money, and it seems that London is now the money-laundering capital of the world. While it is popular to talk about the Russians and Chinese as the main people who benefit from laundering their ill-gotten gains in London's prime central housing market, the sad fact is that this has been favoured by British Criminals and Slum Landlords for decades too, as well as corrupt public figures. There is a famous slum Landlord who is supposedly a self-made billionaire, primarily because he started out exploiting the Land and property laws in the 1960s to his own advantage to the detriment of tenants, who also uses offshore tax structures to avoid paying pretty much any tax at all. He is just one example of the kind of person who uses the property market to accumulate vast wealth while adding no productivity to the economy.

If this book does become popular, then I do expect a certain amount of character-assassination on the part of some politicians, the professional elite and the media that they influence. After all, they are the vested interests in keeping the affordability of housing on an ever-downward trend, and they stand to lose out the most by making long-term house prices more affordable.

We all like to believe in a conspiracy theory or two, they are part of modern life. Whether it is the 'real' cause of the Spanish-American war or the goings-on in WW2, we can all find a conspiracy out there we like the idea of. Rather than condemn or condone conspiracy theories, I believe that widespread belief in conspiracy theories by society these days should really be taken as a *symptom* that there are major things wrong with the way a country is working, and the direction that country is taking. In other words, if something is so badly wrong with the way a society works, that people feel they have no choice but to believe in conspiracy theory that created that situation, then that is a symptom of the underlying problem in society. And so therefore that a society needs to fix certain major aspects of how it works. I, and probably most of the UK, now believe that serious long-term action needs to be taken to fix the UK housing market. I believe there is a link between the rise of conspiracy theories in America, Britain and the other 'Anglo-Saxon' countries since the early 1990s, and the increasing inequality of wealth in our countries, the social inequality. The solution could involve rolling back most of the laws affecting Land and property that have accumulated since the 2nd World War.

I hope that you find this book illuminating/enlightening and that it opens your eyes to what has been happening in our society since the end of World War 2. If it is allowed to continue, then we will end up in some kind of neo-feudalistic society of neo-serfdom. And clearly this is a trend that must be stopped and reversed, as has happened in the past. The housing crisis is near breaking point in this country, and the social tension since the Brexit vote is still present, despite most people coming to terms with the vote. There is still a sense that there are fundamental things wrong with your society.

My own experience of the housing market in our country has been one of frustration. It always appears to be a Sellers market… and they just seem to be able to get away with charging alot of money for dilapidated buildings and Land. For this reason I am finding myself struggling to find reasons to stay here, and am seriously considering moving to a country where I can afford to live in a much better home, or better still build one for myself without paying through the nose for Land.

In other countries in Europe and around the world, they let you build houses, sometimes practically anywhere you want. If you want to build in the countryside, they let you do that. But in Britain, they don't. We lack this Fundamental Freedom, this Liberty in our lives, to settle.

And this has been going on for almost 70 years, and in virtually no other countries too.

One of the amazing things I have noticed about the book market and the information media in general in our country, is that there are no books or works on the state of the housing market. I couldn't find anything on Amazon. Which is very odd, considering the importance of the issue. It's very Bizarre, that what is one of the top 3 issues in our society today has almost no publicly available literature on it. There are books available on trying to get planning permission and the physical process of building your own home (so these books are clearly responding to the dream of building our own home), but there are no books on the actual real underlying political and economic issue of house prices. Which is Bizarre, seeing that this is less of a taboo subject than say, Immigration was before the EU Vote. This is discussed in public and in the media - but the debate does not go anywhere near deep enough and it *is* taboo to state the real causes.

So here it is, the first book that really takes a look at the housing market from the current perspective and relative perspectives of the wider political and economic issues of the 21st century.

But back to the core issue in this book. So, why are house prices so high? The price of any commodity, or asset, or thing, can be divided into and is governed by, its constituent factors of Supply and Demand. So what I seek to do in the next 2 chapters is to present the factors to you that influence the Supply and Demand of property in the UK. The content is by no means exhaustive, as I only have a limited amount of time to write this book. But I do intend to provide the meat behind my argument.

CHAPTER 2
SUPPLY

This chapter of the book is concerned with laying out the drivers of house prices that affect the Supply of Houses. As some of you may know, it has been recognised that the primary cause of high prices has been a lack of supply of houses. But *Why* is there a lack of supply of new houses? What are the underlying causes of this? I am about to show you. But first an update of the UK economy since the Brexit vote.

THE CURRENT ECONOMIC SITUATION IN THE UK

As of Christmas 2016, a lot has happened in a relatively short space of time in the UK economy. The result of the UK independence referendum was that we voted to leave the EU. And most importantly, of the countries making up the UK, England and Wales voted to leave the EU by a firm majority.

The immediate result of the leave result was a sharp fall in the value of the pound, also known as 'Sterling'. Stock Markets fell, but then quickly rose again. However, the Pound has stayed low. This has had important implications for Inflation, and may have important implications for house prices. The falling pound brings with it huge risks to our way of life in this country. It could eventually lead to an economic collapse if interest rates to do not rise, via a death spiral in the pound, that would make it easier for rich foreigners to use their wealth to 'buy up' sections of the UK economy, attaching onerous conditions, pushing us further towards neo-serfdom. I shall talk more about neo-Serfdom later. The Pound has been destabilised by its move outside of its recent historical trading range. I suggest that this is likely to trigger serious imbalances that have been building within our society and our economy for a number of decades. This is potentially very dangerous for us.

Really, the UK economy has been treading water ever since the financial crisis of 2007-2009. And all that time house prices have been allowed to soar, because of the 'emergency' interest rate policy of low rates and money-printing. The pound's fall has now triggered the bursting of the bond bubble, and there could be a great self-reinforcing liquidation of all uk assets. And given the UK is such an important financial centre, this would have huge implications for the world economy and would probably cause another financial crisis.

Mark Carney, the Governor of the Bank of England, has spoken about the need for supply-side reform of britain. I suspect he is referring to the Land and property law.

PLANNING LAW AND THE TOWN AND COUNTRY PLANNING ACT 1947, 1954, 1990 & 2008

The history of Planning Law in this country dates back primarily to the Town and Country Planning Act 1947. This was a law that was brought in by the post-war Labour Government, and it introduced for the first time the concept that you had to apply for planning permission if you wanted to build a house or make changes to existing buildings. Before this law was brought in, you didn't need to seek permission from anyone if you wanted to build a house, anywhere. That's right, if you had the Money and the Will, you could literally pitch up anywhere in the countryside, buy some Land, and put a house there. You were only limited by what was achievable practically and technologically, such as steep slopes, soil type, and the limitations of materials transportation etc, but historically people tended to naturally settle close to food and water sources. When the 1947 act was brought in, this Fundamental Freedom disappeared. The 1947 Act, in effect, nationalised the right to develop Land. No compensation was given to Landowners for taking this right away from them. It was appropriated by Law.

A little backdrop is necessary to explain this. The feeling and climate in society at the time, around World War 2, was that of a mindset of command

and control, and totalitarianism, a desire to control what people did in their lives, and an acceptance of that control for the common good, which stemmed from the war era. World War 2 required strict planning and control of what was done in the national economy on a scale never achieved before, in order to stand a chance of being on the winning side. And this thought extended to town and city planning, to such an extent that it was deemed that people had to apply for permission even to build houses. All Western countries were playing at Command and Control, not just Hitler and Stalin, they all brought in laws at very similar times. Except that Britain's planning laws have evolved over time to be the most restrictive in the world.

One of the ideas behind the introduction of the planning law in the late 1940s, was that with a lot of people having nowhere to live in the bombed-out aftermath of the War, it was thought at the time that the government was in the best position to take charge of the rebuilding effort and control it on a national scale, because it was thought that the market was not capable enough to achieve this rebuilding itself in a short space of time. The same rationale was also used to keep Food Rationing until relatively late compared to Europe, rather than let the free market respond to high food prices with increased supply.

Below is an extract of the Planning Policy contained in the Planning Law of this country. It's important that you read this.

LOCAL PLAN/LOCAL DEVELOPMENT FRAMEWORK POLICIES FOR NEW HOUSES

Proposals for housing development will be permitted:
Within settlement boundaries provided that the proposal is for the re-use, renovation or redevelopment of previously developed Land or buildings on sites within the settlements. In addition, proposals for the following will be permitted on greenfield sites:

(a) The development of small sites, 0.4 hectare or less within the settlements; or

(b) Schemes to provide affordable housing which meet the requirements of policy HS13

Outside Planning Boundaries planning permission for new residential

development will be *refused* unless:
(a) It is in conformity with the criteria detailed in HS11 (Rural exceptions policy), or
(b) It is demonstrated by the applicant that there is a clearly established existing functional need for an enterprise to be in a countryside location, there is a proven need for someone to live on site, and that the enterprise is economically viable.

Within defined built-up areas, permission will be given to proposals for residential development where the following criteria are met:
(a) The development does not involve the significant loss of an area of natural conservation or an open or wooded area of Land;
(b) The Land or building is not within an established business area and is not allocated for any other use in this Local Plan;
(c) Efficient use is made of the Land in terms of density and as general guidance should be provided at a density of at least 30 dwellings per hectare;
(d) The character and form respects that of the locality;
(e) Includes a high quality environment for prospective occupiers including appropriate Landscaping and open space;
(f) The provision for car parking and vehicle maneouvring does not significantly reduce garden areas, including front gardens, or adversely affect adjoining property.

Planning permission will be refused for residential infilling outside the Urban Areas or Defined Settlements unless:
1) The site is a small gap in an otherwise built-up frontage; and
2) The development does not detract from the rural character of the area or result in the loss of attractive views of the countryside; and
3) The proposal does not consolidate existing development in remote areas or those served by unsatisfactory roads.

It is this small part of the planning law, this very small part that has such a profound effect on our society and completely rules out building anywhere outside of the planning boundaries that surround every settlement in our country. The section marked in bold above shows that in order to build a house outside the planning boundaries in our country, to settle outside of a city or town or village, in the 'countryside', you basically have to be in some kind of rural industry such as a farmer or stable-owner.

You can see from this excerpt above that the planning law just seems to be very biased against building houses full stop, in the name of protecting the countryside, nature and conservation areas. I shall talk more about the 'countryside' and what it really is later on.

How does this planning law work? The crux is that the planning law clearly states that planning permission cannot be granted to build houses on Land designated as 'countryside'. The excerpt from the planning law above clearly states that. I have seen this myself in formal written responses to planning applications on the local government planning websites. It just so happens the Land outside planning boundaries constitutes between 80%-95% of the Land in this country, and it has been classed as 'countryside'. *So there is an effective Ban on building on 80%+ of the Land in this country!* The graph of housebuilding in this country shows a clear trend to the downside over the course of many decades, since this law was introduced. It is an undeniable fact that if you ban building on 80%+ of the Land, housebuilding is going to decline as you gradually run out of Building Land.

[GRAPH SHOWING HOUSEBUILDING NUMBERS]

If you want to go outside of a town or city and build a house, to the countryside, where most of the Land actually is, and build a home for yourself, the law will not let you do that. If you want to build a home where most of the physical Land in this country actually is, the planning law does not let you do that. You are not allowed to do that. We are not allowed to do that. And that is the principal reason why not enough homes have been built since the end of the 2nd World War. There is an effective Ban on building on 80%-95% of the Physical Land in Britain, plain and simple.

What is the effect of this on the housing market? By ruling out 80%+ of the Land from ever realistically being built on immediately gets rid of most of the potential supply of building Land, and thus new houses. And by fundamentally restricting the supply of new houses, or any other asset that humans have a basic need for, you are guaranteeing long-term rising house prices. And I don't just mean prices rising in line with inflation in the wider economy. I mean ever-rising prices, with the eventual result that houses become progressively less affordable for each new generation that comes of age and tries to enter the housing market. This is the real and primary reason why not enough homes have been built for several decades now. It is because the supply has been artificially restricted.

But the Planning Law actually negatively Rigs the Land Market and thus the Housing Market in more than just 1 way, it does it in several ways. I will explain:

1. The outright 80%+ reduction in the amount of potential building Land via the use of planning boundaries restricting the supply of new housing, therefore…
2. Causing high building Land prices through the scarcity of building Land, which means that Builders have to over-leverage (take out larger loans) to pay for the Land in order to carry on their house-building business, *making them vulnerable to economic recessions and financial crises… An example is the last financial crisis of 2007-2009 permanently taking many smaller builders out of the market…*
3. Eventually raising Land prices so much, so that after builders go bust in the previous recessions and financial crises, the next generation of builders (from our generation) cannot come into the building trade to replace and replenish housing supply, because the barriers to entry are too high in the form of, yes you guessed it, Land prices!

And so you can see how the Rigging of the supply of Building Land has effect after effect downstream of the immediate effect of restricting the supply of Land, that work together to fundamentally reduce the long term supply of houses by making builders go bust and new ones (us) from coming in. Cause and Effect.

This shows how the Land and Housing Market in our country is a classic economics textbook example of a market that is Broken through 70 years of government intervention. And mostly in the selfish pursuit of ever-rising house prices.

By restricting all housing development to taking place inside or very near to existing town and city planning boundaries also means a huge advantage to big corporations who can afford to buy up the Land that has been made expensive by an artificially restricted supply of building Land. This is because as Land prices rise, they act as a barrier to entry for smaller housebuilders and individuals and families who are industrious and want to create a new home for themselves. This high cost as a barrier to entry has actually permeated our entire society and is beginning to have huge effects on the current and future competitiveness of our country compared to the rest of the world. It impacts the startup costs for a young person trying to start their own business. We simply cannot get the money together to start a business, and a sacrifice has to be made between owning a home or starting a business. But as I will reveal later in the book, any attempt by the big housebuilders to bring in more housing supply may well result in them going bust and reducing the long-term housing supply even further.

The effect this has on the economy is profound. Once you pass a law that persistently restricts the supply of new housing, even as old houses decay and become unsuitable for modern habitation, you are not able to replace them with more modern dwellings in sufficient numbers. And so our quality of life relative to other western countries falls.

There are even villages and hamlets outside of cities which have no official designation as settlements, so that it is unclear that the houses in those settlements will be allowed to be rebuilt if they were to fall down or be destroyed, even people who may have lived there for hundreds of years.

In the context of it's time, the 1947 act and all of its constituent parts was probably really just another way for a Socialist Labour government to control the means of production in our society, alongside nationalising industries, as part of their grand socialist scheme. I understand that Labour and the Unions had a stated policy of Land nationalisation in the 1970s. This was the era of totalitarian government control and the Soviet Union. Labour was trying to create it's statist vision of the future and attempting to create as communist a state as it could.   Nationalising industries and controlling planning & development was part of their grand socialist scheme.   Later, Tory governments left the planning laws in place, as they probably quickly realised that the rising Land and property prices it created raised the values of theirs and their rural supporters' homes and Land holdings, and secured the votes of the 'countryside' movement.

Is it a coincidence that at just the time when Cars were becoming more available, and construction technology was being industrialised, so living in countryside was becoming easier and more appealing than it ever has been; And so planning laws have been introduced to stop us doing just that! To stop us from realising our dreams of owning our own piece of England!

Other countries have planning law to stop you building in the wilderness because great parts of it are uninhabitable or are outright Desert. We do not have these issues in our country. The vast majority of our Land is habitable, proven by it being oh so 'full of life' and 'green and pleasant', as the countryside movement likes to say! So if Life thrives in our countryside, surely that means that we humans can thrive out there too? You can start to see the Hypocrisy in our Land Laws.

In addition to the restrictions on where you can build, the planning law also makes sure that there is a huge amount of bureaucracy in the planning process. This means that it can take years to get planning permissions for housing developments, while public consultations and risk assessments get carried out at as slow a pace as possible. And so it takes years to get anything done. I argue that the entire Public consultations process itself is biased in favour of Nimbys and their views. This is because the kind of people who oppose housing developments are just the kind of people who have a lot of spare time on their hands in order to do so, whereas the people who are in favour of housing developments tend to be hard-working families who are too busy with their lives to find much time to support the development process. I will talk further about the Nimbys and their detrimental impact later on.

The bottom line is that the law of our Land and our government just does not like housebuilding, *fullstop*.

Over time the original 1947 Planning Act has been replaced and superseded by other Planning Acts... all of these have further tightened the Planning Law.

My statements about the UK Planning System are central to my argument about why UK house prices are so high, about why in some places they are almost double what they should be.

This law is the single biggest factor affecting the supply of housing in our country. This concept of Planning boundaries that wrap around all the settlements in our country, serves to restrict where you can build a house. Building inside the Planning Boundaries is a very bureaucratic process, while building outside is impossible and is treated as though it is a violation of sacred Land and law! The overall impact is that the supply of building Land in this country is *Rigged*.

1955 GREEN BELT DESIGNATION

The next stage in our journey through the housing market laws that have affected house prices is the Green Belt. In 1955, a government circular was spread around Whitehall. This circular stated that from that moment on, the ring of Land surrounding each of the UK's major or historic cities would be essentially be sectioned off and used as a barrier to development. This time around, it was a Conservative goverment that enacted these changes. In all likelihood they saw what the earlier introduction of Planning Permission had done to house prices, and the differential it created between Agricultural Land and Residential Land, and decided that they wanted more of that. It is not easy to draw that conclusion though. In fact, Green Belts had existed around London and other cities even earlier. The Green Belts around London, Birmingham and Sheffield were among the first to be established in the 1930s.

Green belts were created to aim to stop 'urban sprawl' where cities in particular such as London and Birmingham were expanding outwards at huge rates which was leading to haphazard development which among other things was clogging up the roads. It also aimed to stop the merging of neighbouring settlements into single large towns, and 'preserve the character of historic towns' and encourage development to locate within existing built-up areas. The quality or appearance of Land is not a factor in its designation as green belt and it does not have to be "green". It can be any piece of Land, even a run-down industrial site or a disused waste ground.

The effect of all this is to further restrict where houses can be built by 'locking in' development to take place inside planning boundaries and giving them no way to expand slowly over time. Green belt policy is just another chance to restrict development, in the name of 'protecting' the 'sacred' countryside at all costs. It is an addition to the original planning acts that restricts the supply of building Land, therefore pushing up long term house prices. In fact, the stated aim of Green Belts is just that, to stop development. Given that London is by far our largest city, with the highest population and a growing one, and yet has a very large Green Belt, this clearly shows the obsessive government policy of stopping house building full stop.

Green belts are now so large and wide, stretching out into the countryside, that they effectively stop most building occurring anywhere in the counties adjacent to the cities they are supposed to be 'protecting'.

The Wikipedia page on Green Belts has the following statement:

"Green belt policy has been criticised for reducing the amount of Land available for building and therefore pushing up house prices, as 70% of the cost of building new houses is the purchase of the Land (up from 25% in the late 1950s)."

This statement effectively backs up my argument that restricting which Land can be built on severely reduces the supply of building Land and therefore new houses. And this is just the part on Greenbelt. It says nothing about the much larger impact of the Planning Boundaries ruling out 80%-95% of the Land from ever being built on. It shows that there are others out there who agree with my view that the supply of building Land is Rigged in our country.

Even the word 'Green Belt' has a marketing feel about it, a deliberately chosen word, that is evocative of the the so-called sacred countryside espoused by the countryside movements. Oh countryside, we worship thee, with thy soft crumbly soil and badger-shit strewn about forest floors. It's sacred, apparently. No, really. If the countryside is so sacred, then why are we not allowed to live there? I will talk more about the countryside later on.

The Nimbys often like to say that 'we need green spaces' in our towns and suburbs. But the reason that developers want to build on these 'Green Spaces' is precisely *because* it impossible to build outside the planning boundaries in the first place, so they are forced to resort to trying to develop the green spaces *inside* the planning boundaries in the towns and cities. And the Green Belt sitting around many towns and cities to stop them expanding, is responsible for this.

https://en.wikipedia.org/wiki/Green_belt_(United_Kingdom)

AREAS OF OUTSTANDING NATURAL BEAUTY

In this section I really want to debate (nail) this phrase, the meaning of it, and its relevance to our countryside. Areas of Outstanding Natural Beauty are a concept and a phrase used by the Government to denote a swathe of countryside that is supposedly so especially pleasant that it also warrants special protection to ensure it is still there in the future. Even though the Planning Law already bans building on the countryside, apparently these areas require a double layer of protection to stop almost all forms of building occurring. I will show you how little meaning this phrase actually has in the context of our 'countryside'.

Let's talk about the impact man has had on the countryside. When modern humans first came to Britain after the ice-age, we started to have a major impact on the Land that was to become the 'countryside' even then. Back then, the Land was covered in trees and the hunter gatherers and then the first farmers began chopping down the trees for farming space and firewood. This clearly has a fundamental impact on the Land. Not only does it change the appearance from Forests to Fields, but the removal of trees and their stabilising roots also makes the soil liable to shift and heave over time as it readjusts to a new equilibrium. This changes the overall appearance of the Land further. It means that man has an impact not just on the appearance of the Land, but also the very structure of the Land itself. Moving onto the Medieval period and the Renaissance, the Forests were further cut back, and Land was subdivided into Fields separated by hedgerows. This further altered the appearance and the very lay of the Land. In the Renaissance and Enlightenment periods, we saw building technology progress so that nicer and better quality buildings and architecture were able to be lived in. This dramatically changed the appearance of dwellings, and thus the Landscape and countryside. With the Industrial Revolution and 20th Century Industrialism, you saw the rise of Railways, Cars and the Roads that carried them. So Mankind has been altering the Landscape for his use for thousands of years. Which means most of it cannot be called 'natural'. And yet there is this view imposed on society by the Establishment that the countryside must be protected (i.e. not built on) because it is 'natural'. Some people almost see the countryside as 'sacred'. It isn't - we created it.

In order for us to further criticise the concept of AONBs, we need to dissect each constituent word in 'AONB'. When we do this, we can start see how this policy does not stand up to scrutiny.

The word first word 'Area' is reasonable enough to use. It is descriptive of the geographical Landscape covered by the designation. It needs to be used in order for the law behind it to be effective.

The 2nd word is 'Outstanding'. Are AONBs 'Outstanding'? Not much of it all, most of it is very much the same as the rest of the countryside, and it is positively man-made. If you ever go on a drive through the countryside, it all starts to look the same remarkably quickly.

Is it 'Natural'? No, most of it is man-made, only a very small proportion of it is still in its Natural state of ancient forest.

Is it 'Beautiful'? Again, if most of it looks the same, and Beauty is a relative concept, then it cannot all be 'Beautiful'. Beauty is supposed to be individual and rare in character. Very few man-made scenes are beautiful. So why then have vast swathes of the countryside in the South East of England been designated as 'Areas of Outstanding Natural Beauty'? Whether a particular piece of countryside is beautiful or not is largely down to your individual opinion. For every person who feels it looks lovely and special, and gets 'emotional' about it, there is another who merely sees an ugly looking field with a dead badger under a bush, where you get stuck in the mud whenever it rains, which could potentially be used to solve the housing crisis. Oh, and the rain means that the countryside is only truly enjoyable for a few months each year in the Summer, and even the Summer is so unreliable in this country to make this tenuous at best. Remember the Summer Washout of 2012? Or 2007 before that?

The countryside is not sacred. The countryside scenery and view is very much a man-made phenomenon. The layout of the fields, the way they are divided by hedgerows, and the copses and forests scattered between them, these were all designed and laid out by man hundreds of years ago. If Britain was truly natural, most of it would be covered in forest. And yet, the government has designated large swathes of the countryside 'areas of outstanding natural beauty'.

The countryside activists who campaigned for the AONBs got their wishes because the governments of the day realised that bringing this piece of legislation into law would give them an excuse to bring in tight controls over what building took place in these areas, thus restricting the supply of building Land even further, thus further pushing up house and Land prices. It also helped secure the vote of the countryside for the Conservatives.

My point is that Man has been altering the Landscape in our country for thousands of years, to the extent that its current visual condition and Impact is almost entirely man-made. So if the countryside has been created by man, and has historically been in a state of flux, then why are we not allowed to alter it nowadays in other ways? In the name of preserving its 'Outstanding Natural Beauty', which I have just argued is an Ironic Misnomer. It does not stand up to scrutiny. The practical reality of the situation is that the countryside's appearance is always going to change as we progress through time, simply because of the needs of we humans who use it for our own purposes, such as farming, living. The idea of creating Areas of Outstanding Natural Beauty and protecting the countryside is mostly hypocrisy and very ironic given that it is man-made anyway. It is meaningless to create these areas when the countryside is man-made anyway, and the long-term price that is paid in non-development, infringement of human rights, and house prices is too heavy. To create laws that make the countryside 'sacred' is effectively to deny the natural economic and societal progress of man, by stopping economic development from taking place in the natural way that it would occur! It is as if some people are desperately trying to deny this country its economic progress, which is unnatural and destructive. Most of us have put up with it because it is the system we have grown up in, we don't live in the countryside and do not realise the profound effect it has on our economic status.

The countryside needs new blood anyway otherwise it will decay. And we need the Freedom to live outside town 'boundaries' and 'city limits'. Planning boundaries are a relic of a bygone era of statist planning control and totalitarianism. Letting individuals settle where we choose does not mean that huge housing estates are going to crop up out of nowhere that will blight the 'sacred' countryside. It's a ridiculous notion perpetrated by people with vested interests and too much time on their hands.

DIVORCE LAW

Try not to laugh. Yes, I know, I am seriously trying to suggest that even the divorce law in this country conspires to stop houses from being sold, thus restricting supply. It might sound strange, this part, but please hear me out.

Now, I do not want to claim that the only reason that the House often gets transferred into the mother's name during a divorce settlement is because the government doesn't want it to get sold. Clearly the needs of the children to have a stable roof over their heads is fairly important. But it does look strange how the law tries to stop the house getting sold at any cost, even to the point of transferring it solely into the wife's name, supposedly for the benefit of the children. If it was truly about the benefit of the children, then why isn't the house transferred into the childrens name, instead of remaining in the parents hands? In the form of a trust that the parents are made to pay the mortgage on? After all, it's the children who are let down the most by divorce, so why aren't they getting some form of financial compensation for loss of family and poor parenting?

The reduced supply from the divorce is another, albeit small factor, in creating an environment of rising house prices.

Rising house prices have created an incentive for divorce, in that the high value of houses acts as an incentive for the weaker financial party, the dependent (often the wife), to divorce the husband for financial gain. The value of the house plays a part in tempting the spouse to believe that they can get rid of the other spouse and survive alone. With around 50% of marriages ending in divorce these days, the divorce process of splitting assets but trying to stop the 'family home' from being sold wherever possible, has an undeniable effect of keeping the 99% of us divided, weak and fighting each other in society.

NIMBYISM

No book on the causes of the Housing Crisis would be complete without a whole section dedicated to the phenomenon of Nimbyism. Nimby stands for 'Not In My Back Yard'. For those of our generation who do not know what a Nimby is, here is the definition:

What is a Nimby? The definition according to the first result on a Google search is as follows:
Nimby
ˈnɪmbi/
noun
informal
plural noun: **Nimbys**

1. a person who objects to the siting of something perceived as unpleasant or hazardous in their own neighbourhood, especially while raising no such objections to similar developments elsewhere.
2. "rural development arouses intense suspicion from Nimbys and Conservationists"

So immediately we can see that Nimbyism is a form of Hipocrisy.

It gathered pace in the mid-20th century when country houses were being knocked down and being left to go to rack and ruin. For several decades now, whenever somebody or some people in any localities want to build a house or houses, you can always guarantee that so many local residents will come out against the proposal. They throw their hands up in horror at the prospect of somebody, 'who may not even be from around here', building houses near where *they* live. Upon hearing about the proposal to build, they immediately meet up and organise with the utmost urgency, with the aim of stopping the development.

These people are quite often of a certain demographic and age-group. They have a lot of time on their hands, otherwise how would they have the time to so vigorously organise themselves against the developments that they oppose? I myself have been to public consultations and public planning meetings, and seen with my own eyes the general type of people who attend and object to these proposals. They are almost never young. They are almost always elderly or they are usually retired; or they are female home-makers. And the vast majority of them vote for the Conservative Party.

When you look at the type of person who is a Nimby, they are generally the type of person who is a burden on society and does not contribute much to the economy. They are Retirees, and Homemakers. And they like to think that the world owes them something despite not doing much at all themselves. They typically are not very Economically Productive in society in the same way we are or will be. So why does their voice count for so much? They have less stake in the future of our country than we do.

Nimbys have an advantage over pro-housing people, due to lots of spare time, as Nimbys are usually Homemakers, or Semi-retired and Retired. And in addition to having the time to engage in their activism, while those of us who need houses to be built are too busy working because we are actually the economically ones in society, their fervour and belief motivates them to be well-organised to try and stop any and all forms of development. I do not know a single Nimby from our own generation.

When you scrutinise what Nimbys are trying to stop, it is the Creative process. They are aiming to stop people's Desire for Creativity. This is psychologically negative and a Bad Thing. Therefore Nimbyism is illogical and irrational and goes against human instinct. It betrays an irrational and illogical over-emotional mind. They are also incredibly selfish and appear to have no genuine empathy for the situation that our generation is in.

And these are the people who were able to get into the property market decades ago when prices were still cheap. It's alright for them, but they cannot possibly comprehend what it is like for our generation to not be able to afford houses, Basic Shelter. We must drown out the voice of the Nimbys.

We can also see that Nimbys are people who tend to live in affluent sections of the community, who always hold more sway with local councils. And this can be seen by Councils often bowing to the pressures set upon them by these people to site new developments elsewhere. Unless of course they will make their community 'more amenable'. In other words, more desirable, thus *increasing their house prices*. Yes, the main motivation behind Nimbys opposing developments is because they are obsessed with their house prices, and they cling to mostly phantom stories and tales of how developments elsewhere have somehow 'ruined' local house prices. And then use that as a justification to vigorous opposition to housing development. They know that if they are vocal and loud enough, louder than other, poorer communities in their locality, then they will succeed in pushing the proposed development elsewhere. I wonder how Nimbys would feel about a development if was going to *increase* their house prices?

My argument here has been about working toward the idea that Nimbys are mainly affluent people with too much time on their hands, of certain socio-demographics and voter types, and who may be obsessed with ever-rising house prices. And a great portion of them live in the South East of England. These people have no moral standpoint in our society. They do not care about our society. I am glad to have exposed them for what they really are.

LISTED PROPERTIES

What is a Listed Property? Let's take a look at the Wikipedia definition.

"A **Listed building** or **Listed structure**, in the United Kingdom, is one that has been placed on the Statutory List of Buildings of Special Architectural or Historic Interest."

Really, what the government has done, has protected the status of around 400,000 old buildings, with the effect that these buildings cannot be modernised. Their design is often so dated that making changes to their interiors and exteriors is prohibitively expensive, for example just to introduce insulation into these houses. Many of these buildings are not really fit for modern habitation in the 21st century sense of the word, and some of them command very high prices. This is despite the poor design i.e. too much space given over to windows and roofing, meaning a vast bill when these items need to be replaced.

Even the houses of parliament (Palace of Westminster) is so dated, so complex, and so expensive to maintain that people are now saying that if it wasn't a Grade 1 Listed Building then it would be demolished. That is how much of a burden the building now is. The Government is going to have to move out of it for years, to allow it to be refurbished. It's going to cost us billions. And to be honest it is not even attractive, and it's less than 200 years old.

What long term benefits do Listed buildings actually give to our society? They provide us with actual historical examples of the way of life and architecture that existed hundreds of years ago. Yes, we need to preserve some historic buildings to enable us to learn about our past, etc, but 400,000 buildings being Listed? It's more of a burden on society than a benefit.

But who will buy them? Because we certainly won't! My generation just does not have the money to buy these things, or the money to maintain them, but also… these buildings are not good enough for us. They are not fit for 21st century habitation, they do not have proper insulation if they have any at all. I would not touch a Listed building with a barge pole, unless i could get it de-Listed and demolished or fundamentally altered, and even then I wouldn't pay much for it.

I am not saying that certain buildings should not be protected. But I do question the infringement of human rights in making the law that protects them so restrictive that the owners of them cannot update them to modern standards. Many of them are, after all, *peoples homes.*

I predict that most of these Listed buildings will eventually be de-Listed, to make way for them being fundamentally updated and brought up to 21st century standards of living, or demolished.

https://en.wikipedia.org/wiki/Listed_building

RENTIER CAPITALISM

Our housing market is riddled with Rentier Capitalism and the rent-seeking that is prevalent in our housing market.

For those who are unfamiliar with the term, here is the Wikipedia definition:

Rentier capitalism is a term currently used to describe the belief in economic practices of monopolization of access to any (physical, financial, intellectual, etc.) kind of property, and gaining significant amounts of profit without contribution to society.[1][2][3][4] The origins of the term are unclear; it is often said to be used in Marxism, yet the very combination of words rentier and capitalism was never used by Karl Marx himself.

It results in outright transfers of wealth from the many, often real economically people in society, to the few, without generating any form of economic productivity or wealth creation or increase in the overall standard of living of the country. In fact, the many often end up working harder to sustain their living standards to make up for their wealth and standard of living lost in the wealth transfer to the few. I say that this is exactly what is happening in the Western World today.

That unless reversed will become permanent.

In 21st century Britain, Rentier Capitalist should perhaps be defined as follows:

A person who invests in assets with the aim of making abnormal economic profits with little or no economic contribution or creation.

In economics and in public-choice theory, **rent-seeking** involves seeking to increase one's share of existing wealth without creating new wealth. Rent-seeking results in reduced economic efficiency through poor allocation of resources, reduced actual wealth creation, lost government revenue, increased income inequality,[1] and (potentially) national decline.

This is pretty much exactly what has been happening in the housing market here in the UK.

While the main example in our society is the buy-to-let housing market, the one particular example I will show here is the slum-Landlording form where a Landlord will buy up rundown and therefore cheap property in city centres such as Manchester. They then proceed to subdivide the property into as many rooms as possible, and they then fill them with DSS tenants. The reason they do this is because DSS tenants, who will have their the portion of their benefits that are used to pay the rents, get paid directly into the Landlord's bank account. This is to so the tenants do not waste the money on other things and ensures the rent gets paid, which is logical enough. By focussing on filling these rundown properties up with DSS tenants, they guarantee an income stream that has a very high yield. This form of Landlording can yield a return on investment of over 50%! This is one example of the extreme rent-seeking that you see in the buy-to-let market.

CHAPTER 3
DEMAND

In this chapter I will show the main factors that are affecting the *Demand* for Housing in our country. In each section I will comment on how these factors affect house prices in the overall context of the supply restrictions outlined in Chapter 2.

QUANTITATIVE EASING (QE)

What is Quantitative Easing? According to the Bank of England's own website, Quantitative Easing (QE) "is an unconventional form of monetary policy where a Central Bank creates new money electronically to buy financial assets, like Government Bonds. This process aims to directly increase private sector spending in the economy and return inflation to target." This really means that the Central Bank, in our case the Bank of England literally creates money out of thin air and then uses it to buy Government Bonds and other assets it deems 'suitable'.

Central Banks undertook QE to respond to the financial crisis. After using their traditional technique of stimulating the economy by lowering interest rates (and thus encouraging us to take on more debt), to boost spending and investment in the economy (they make a dangerous assumption here that increasing debt is a good thing for us!). Because all they care about is the economy, and their pockets. There is a theory that economic crises are responsible for World Wars etc, and therefore keeping the economy strong at all costs to stop another World War, but the reasons for World Wars are much more complex than that. Inter-Tribal Competition for resources etc is a natural part of the European way of life, and is a natural cause of wars. They found that when they lowered interest rates to near zero, they ran out of room to stimulate the economy in the normal way, because interest rates can only go so low, to near zero. After that was exhausted, they had to think of other ways to stimulate the economy, and so they came up with the idea of QE. This involved creating money out of thin air via creating electronic bank balances, and then using that money to purchase the Government's Bonds on the Financial Markets. It does this in the hundreds of billions of pounds. At last count the amount of Bonds the Bank of England had bought was £475billion. With money it created out of thin air.

What has been the effect of this? What are the money flows in our economy? The immediate effect of purchasing Bonds is to increase the price of those Bonds via increased Demand on the Financial Markets. When the price of a Bond increases, the effective interest rate paid on that Bond falls, because there is an inverse relationship of a Bond's price to its Interest Rate Yield, its income. If interest rates on the government's bonds fall, then it becomes cheaper for the government to borrow money in the future, because the market uses the low interest rates on existing Bonds to price new ones the government wants to issue. If the government is able to borrow at lower interest rates, then the rest of society can too. That means companies and consumers like you and me. And so interest rates on mortgages fall, making mortgages more affordable, meaning you and I can borrow more money to buy a house. And if we borrow more money to buy a house, we can afford to pay a higher price. And because the supply of housing is restricted, sellers find it much easier to demand we pay higher prices. So house prices rise.

Again, in the environment of a restricted supply, QE just lowers interests much further than they otherwise would be, and so has just boosted house prices even further. This is reinforced because the supply element of the housing market is so broken, that it cannot respond to increasing prices by building more houses, thus reinforcing the Rigged Market.

QE has really only boosted the value of property and bonds. And given that this effect has lasted for years, it must have been apparent to The Establishment Elite. So why did they keep on doing it? It is as if the Bank of England is so desperate to keep house prices going up like the rest of the political-economic elite and the chattering classes, to make them so unaffordable, that they are willing to throw everything they have at it. Even though Brexit has not really resulted in a recession, they still lowered interest rates and boosted QE. It doesn't make any sense. Why? It starts to makes sense if they were scared about house prices and wanted to keep them going up. On the subject of that interest rate cut in August 2016, public opinion and commentators are now widely criticising it as being just another excuse to lower interest rates. People believe the Bank of England has made a big mistake. And that interest rate cut was swiftly followed by a new fall in the value of sterling. And the implication behind the scenes, is that they did this to support house prices. So one has to wonder just how far the Bank of England wants to go to support house prices. Will they sacrifice sterling in a desperate attempt to support house prices and keep their personal equity intact, and allow them time to pay down their huge mortgages?

Yes, there are 'structural' problems with property in this country. But why hasn't the government acted sooner? Why no tax on property gains to take the demand out? Instead they bring in the 'help the buy' scheme, which only encourages demand and does nothing for supply. It is as if the Elite is determined to lock the younger generation into permanently higher prices.

So, to summarise, the Bank of England has deliberately inflated house prices by using fake money created out of thin air to lower the interest rates we borrow our mortgages at. It has done this on the auspices of 'stimulating the economy'. And this is not just my opinion, this has becomewidely accepted as fact by commentators, financial markets workers and politicians all over the world.

QE creates winners and losers, and increases division in our society, and should be wound down. There have been winners and losers from loose Global Monetary Policy. It's not obvious what the last few years of QE have done to help us. The longer it has gone, the more winners and losers it has created.

The Governors of the Bank of England can never claim to be independent in their decision-making, simply because by owning houses themselves, they are participants in the tax-free Housing Market, and have a huge conflict of interest in their multi-million pound houses and the mortgages attached to them. They will look for *any excuse* imaginable to keep interest rates low and house prices rising, and when their current excuse is no longer valid or tenable, they will just come up with a new one. As an example, look how quickly they lowered interest rates soon after the Brexit vote, even though the economy turned out to be much stronger than thought, and so didn't need a rate cut. They waited a month, yes, but I suspect that was just for form's sake. The bottom line is *interest rates went down*! Their reason was so-called expected weakness in the UK economy after the vote. Now they are even talking about letting inflation rise above their target for years. It's all being done so that they do not have raise interest rates, even though guarding against inflation is the fundamental job of monetary policy! It's bullshit and I am glad that it has now widely been exposed.

I do wonder, if in fact Mark Carney would rather leave his job as Governor rather than raise Interest Rates.

PRINCIPAL PRIVATE RESIDENCE RELIEF

Principal Private Residence Relief is a tax relief, which basically means that we do not have to pay tax on any profit we make on the sale of our home. By profit I mean the difference between the amount you managed to sell it for, minus the total amount you have spent on it, including improvements and extensions etc.

This particular tax relief was sold to us on the basis that what we 'earn' we should keep. That we should keep the money we spend on the roof over our heads. The rationale is that it enables people to retain their housing wealth, thus making it easier to move around the country to follow the work. While this is understandable, the argument becomes tenuous when it contributes to prices rising so much that people are making millions without paying any tax. Despite the fact we are all used to paying 20-40% of our wages away as income tax, apparently it is outrageous that we then should not have to pay capital gains tax on the profit we make from selling our houses, even if that profit is in the millions. That's right - if you are lucky enough to own a house in central London, say Knightsbridge or Chelsea, and this is your 'main' house (i.e. you live in it most of the time), and you sell your house for even £100million, making a profit of £95million because you paid 'only' £5million for it in the 1980s, *you will not have to pay a penny of tax on that £95million profit.* Now, just go through that thought in your head again for a few seconds. And then ask yourself, *does that seem right?*

The effect of this tax is not just to allow people to make ridiculous amounts of money out of property over the short and long term, it serves as an incentive for people and speculators to reinvest that money into the housing market and put even more in on top of that. This is most evident in Central London, of course. *Does that seem right to you?* Is it right that in our society we allow these kinds of gains to be made completely tax-free while most of the rest of us pay our taxes, and those under 40 can't afford to buy houses? The Rich, can speculate in housing as a business and not pay a penny of tax on it, while we cannot even afford to buy a modest house or flat. This is one of the main scandals in 21st century, that this law exists and allows people to escape paying a penny of tax on housing profits of millions of pounds.

It is also one of the main issues that this work seeks to expose. It would actually be very simple to fix this issue. Abolish the PPR relief and tax the capital gains on housing. And to counter the expected counter-argument that it would not be workable to expect everybody who sells a house to fill out the capital gains tax section of the their tax return and complete tax computations, I have a very simple solution. Collect the tax at the point of sale, in the same way that Stamp Duty Land Tax is collected. A simple flat tax of around 20%-40% depending on the gain, can be collected when the sale information is sent off to the Land Registry. The Land Registry collects the tax in the same way as it does with Stamp Duty, and the sale is not recognised under UK law until the tax on difference in bought and sold prices is received. The Solicitor pays it when it pays Stamp Duty. It's simple - if you want your sale of the property to be recognised under UK law, you pay the tax on completion as you do with Stamp Duty. Billions could be collected that way, funding tax cuts in other areas of the economy that would boost economic growth. This rule would also automatically apply to whoever owned the property, whether it's an individual, a family, or a Company. The tax is paid by the seller, whether individual or corporate, on completion of the sale, and the sale is not legally recognised until the tax has been received by the Land registry from whoever sold the property. This stops people evading it as the buyer will not be able to sell the property themselves until the previous seller's solicitor has paid the tax. Acts as an incentive to reinvest money in property.

The only real limit on claiming PPR is not based on the value of the home or the profit made on sale, but on the amount of Land the home sits on. This is about 1 acre, or 0.5 hectares. And given that the vast majority of prime central london homes sit on less than 1 acre, these all potentially qualify for PPR. meaning no tax will be paid on their increase in value over the last 40 years. Which is roughly a factor of at least 10, possibly 20. So as I've already mentioned above, a house in central london bought in the 1970s for £1million, and conservatively worth, lets say, £10million now, will not have a single penny of tax to pay on the £9million profit made. *Does that look right to you?* If we posed this question in a survey to the general public, what would be the result? A clear majority in favour of some kind of tax on the gain of houses, at least to those valuable houses.

The original intention of PPR was to allow private homeowners, the general public, a way to keep their hard-earned wealth that they had ploughed into paying off their mortgage. It was seen as justifiable because people have already been taxed on their income, so why should they be taxed on the asset their earnings have funded? The problem is that assumes that house prices do not rise over the long term. We know they have risen by a factor of 10-20 in 40 years. PPR is also abused by people who are able to choose which of their many houses is their main residence for tax purposes, thus avoiding paying tax on what could be their most valuable asset, worth millions. It is very easy to 'flip' between which house is your main residence. This is what enables prime central london home owners to escape paying tax on their very valuable houses. There are also a myriad of legal reasons that you can justify claiming PPR on your property, even if it isn't your main residence. A quick google search produces a result on the website of a high-end international British estate agency that gives advice on claiming PPR.

PPR doesn't directly stimulate demand for houses. It is does it more indirectly. By allowing people to keep all of what are unnatural economic gains from house price rises, it ensures that all or most of that profit is ploughed back into other house purchases, thus keeping the profit inside the housing market. So PPR works affects the housing market by stopping the removal of house price profits via tax, reducing the movement of capital away from house prices, thus sustaining the upward trend.

A further point I want to make, exposes the mainstream media's collusion in the inequity of PPR. Where in the media, on TV or in the newspapers do you see anybody actually criticise PPR? Where do you see the commentary railing against the tax-free gains that rich people are able to make in property? Is this because they are part of the Establishment Elite purely interested in maintaining the status quo, the vested interests who are making lots of money out of property.

Instead, you see newspapers like The Daily Telegraph argue for the outright abolition of Capital Gains Tax on all assets. And this would mean the same for houses. And what that means is that people will be able to speculate outright in the price of property that isn't even their home, without ever paying a penny of tax on the profits they make! It means that the rich can dump billions of pounds into property on property portfolios, make a lot of of money on the price of it, and then sell it without paying any tax. This would be done on the basic property that you and I find it so hard to afford. This money will then just get ploughed back into property again, having the effect of pushing property prices even higher. And this is the real goal of the Establishment Elite and the Vested Interests from that generation, because they want to go on benefitting from ever-rising house prices while paying little or no tax.

FOREIGN MONEY

The concept of Rich Foreigners moving to and buying property in London is a recent story in our press. Rich Foreigners have been blamed for the astronomical property prices in London, as if it is one of the main reason for high prices. Rich Foreigners are certainly *a* reason, but it seems from the way the opinion has focussed on this as part of the wider anti-immigration debate, that our attention is trying to be distracted from the main overriding reasons, which are a 'stable property market' (ever-rising prices) and easily avoidable Capital Gains Tax.

The context of restricted Land and Property supply in our country means that additional supply cannot be brought into the market to satisfy the additional Demand from wealthy foreigners and immigrants. This means that when the considerable wealth of foreigners moves into the property market it directly pushes up property prices or luxury building projects rather than increasing housing building large supply.

Foreigners like to come to Britain because of the historical guarantee of property rights that this country offers. That means that throughout our history, people's rights to property have been respected, not taken away from them. Other countries supposedly have worse records in this respect, where they have had periodic revolutions and engaged in mass transfers and appropriations of wealth, so Britain looks 'safe' in this respect. But how safe is Britain really? And at what cost to our society? I would say that half of these foreigners do not pay tax on the gains on the properties they buy and sell here, regardless of how high the tax is in their own countries.

Our historic honouring of property rights has gained us a good reputation globally as a safe haven for money. Now, that has been painted by the media, generally the house-price obsessed media, as a positive thing. But is this a good thing, that down the centuries there has never a transfer of Land and assets into the hands of those who can use them best? Or is it just that *we've never had a proper revolution that has resulted in real change for the benefit of the people?* The Norman conquest, by the way, was a revolution of sorts, but that resulted in the most of the Land moving into the hands of Vikings in disguise, away from Anglo-Saxons. It was an appropriation, not a revolution.

Unfortunately however, it has been shown that a lot of the foreign money flowing into the London property market has been Money Laundering. For those who need to know, Money Laundering is the process of transforming the proceeds of crime into clean 'legitimate' assets. It aims to conceal the criminal origin of the money in the process. It is suspected that Money Laundering has played a significant role in pushing up prime central london property prices on the Demand side. Money Launderers are willing to pay a premium over the market price of a property, preferably as an off-market transaction, in order to guarantee the success of that part of the money laundering process. This means that wealthy central londoners are complicit in the Money Laundering process when they sell their properties to Money Launderers.

Now I shall talk about Free Capital Flows. For decades now, the UK economic policy has been for zero restrictions on capital flows into and out of the UK. The Free Market and Capitalist justification for this is that if you place restrictions on capital flowing out of a country, then it may never arrive in the first place as investment flows. This is an oversimplification of the capital flow process. Capital (Money) Flows are affected by many different factors, especially in the UK. In the UK, because the Land and Property supply is restricted by 80%+, most foreign capital flows into the UK property market just push up house prices even more.

I argue that the policy of free capital movement, low interest rates and the wide knowledge among the world's rich of the UK housing market as guaranteed in one direction, has resulted in large flows of foreign money into the UK (London) housing market as speculative flows and house-buying rather than house-building. This has helped push up prices. You can see again, that because Supply has deliberately been restricted for 70 years, that a self-reinforcing long-term rise in house prices has occurred, helped by an influx of suspect foreign money.

While much has been made in the British press about this foreign money and it's murky source, the fact is that it has been going on for decades. The UK property market is one of the world's key places to launder ill-gotten gains. The Global Elite knows that the UK property has been a one-way ticket for many decades, they know about the laws that work together to push up UK house prices, so they know that UK house prices are a one-way bet that it is easy to avoid and evade tax on. They know what is happening to this country and what is behind it.

IMMIGRATION

Mass immigration in Britain is essentially a post-war phenomenon in Britain. It has been going on for the 70 years of post-war history in the UK. Yes, there has obviously been immigration occurring before in the UK's history. But the amount and background of immigration from all over the world has not been seen before in the UK. While Britain before WW2 was a mixture of Germanic and Celtic peoples, its dominating culture, language and genetics was undeniably Germanic and its 'mixture' was that of local North Europeans.

Beginning with Tony Blair, the net migration into this country has soared in recent decades. Blair's 'neoliberal legacy' was carried on by David Cameron.

What is the effect of Immigration on the Housing Market? This is a logical cause and effect. When immigrants come into our country for work or whatever other reason, they will need somewhere to live. For most migrants this will typically be rental accommodation at first. So when migrants enter the rental market looking for a place to live, this will mean more people overall looking for a place to rent; meaning more people compete with each other for that rental, meaning Landlords will be able to raise their prices. This will also have an undeniable effect on house prices too. In the decades after WW2, man of the professional Landlords, and slum Landlords too, played an important role in housing newly arrived immigrants in the cheap property portfolios they were acquiring. 2 particular slum Landlords were well known for this.

In the context of a restricted supply of Building Land and properties, the Demand boost from mass immigration will exacerbate rising house prices all over the country, but most of all in the towns and cities where there is large-scale immigration. That is economic logic.

Immigration is one of the Pillars of the Political 21st century vision for Britain, along with ever-rising house prices. It has been sustained for decades, but like all supposedly 'good' things, this has to come to an end. And then people will realise just how much social and economic division it has created.

PROPERTY BUSINESSES AND OFFSHORE TAX HAVENS

A Tax Haven is defined as a country or independent area where taxes are levied at a low rate relative to other jurisdictions. They often also have strong legal systems guarding privacy and property rights. While the modern concept of the tax haven was formed in the aftermath of World War 1 and the introduction of the Welfare State in Britain, the concept of tax havens actually dates back as far as Ancient Greece, where Sea Traders used to use certain Greek Islands to avoid the 2% trade tax imposed by Athens.

Who uses tax havens? The original users were businessmen who wanted to avoid or evade tax. That changed in the 20th century as families looked to establish trusts offshore to protect family assets and inheritances from tax. After Drugs like Heroin and Cocaine were criminalised during WW1, Drug Traffickers moved underground and started using Tax Havens to hide the nature of their business. Individuals started using tax havens to evade their personal tax obligations, and also to hide assets from their spouses.

What is the effect on the housing market of tax havens? The obvious statement is that they enable developers to avoid taxes. This enables a developer to retain more profit for future reinvestment in their industry which would generally be a good thing for the economy. But this is property development, in a building market where the supply of Land is fundamentally restricted, meaning that the effect of low property taxation will exacerbate the effect of restricted Land supply on rising house prices. Because most of the developers who do this are luxury developers, if the money they make is reinvested, they end up using it to reinvest in more luxury exclusive developments, raising house prices further.

Sadly, while some recent laws have been introduced that levy higher stamp duty on properties bought through companies, this does not touch the profits made on the property. And it is still too easy to use offshore companies and trusts to avoid paying tax on property development full stop. The effect of this is to the same as PPR relief described earlier. It acts as an incentive and allows people to fully reinvest their property profits back into a housing market that has restricted supply, thus virtually guaranteeing high profits. There are 2 British well-known brotherly property developers whose main business has been developing Prime Central London property who are well known to use offshore company structures to avoid or evade paying tax on their profits, mainly through the concept of being able to say that the major decision-making has been taking place offshore rather than in the UK, which under UK tax law means the profits are not taxable under UK law, and so they claim to be within the tax rules when they don't pay any meaningful tax on their luxury development profits.

Most of these offshore tax havens are small countries, often Islands and former colonies, who gained their independence in the post-war era of declining empires. Most of these countries only exist because of the laissez faire attitude of modern western governments towards their tax policies. This offshore tax havens only exist because we allow them to. Because these tax havens are reliant on their closest western sponsors to defend them, they are unable to defend themselves. I would expect that one day the independence of these 'countries' will be rolled back and they will be reabsorbed and reconsolidated into larger nations. For example, Monaco is essentially part of

France, but it only has 'independence' and the Freedom to be a tax haven because France allows it to. France can violate Monaco's sovereignty, fully incorporate it into France, and halt its tax haven status at any time if it wanted to, putting an end to rich celebrities and businessmen using it as a place to live and avoid paying tax on their earnings. Britain can do the same with the Channel Islands, the Isle of Man, and probably a whole bunch of Caribbean Islands if it wanted to by imposing direct rule and changing their tax laws in UK parliament.

It is not yet clear cut whether tax havens will be curtailed or even stopped in the future. It is straightforward to stop them because they are all either small countries that cannot defend themselves, or territories of former empires like the UK. But it is less clear if international competition to attract business and investment will allow low business tax rates to be eliminated. It looks more likely that former countries will re-integrate tax havens into their own economies to get the benefits of low business tax.

There are some good informative websites out there that give good details on how tax havens work and their history. They are worth reading up on. By the way, it would seem that those brotherly property developers I wrote about earlier may well get their comeuppance soon, as some things are coming out in a court case that may well lead to a tax prosecution.

http://www.historyandpolicy.org/policy-papers/papers/history-of-tax-havens

INHERITANCE TAX

Inheritance tax is the only time that most of us pay any tax on the gains on property during our lifetimes.

The Conservative Government recently proposed to remove all family homes worth up to £1million from the net of inheritance tax. Aside from meaning that families pay less inheritance tax when a homeowner dies, the economic effect on the housing market is that less money is extracted from the housing market in the form of tax. As, inheritances usually mostly end up in property anyway, this means that this policy is a way of sustaining high house prices.

This law has been sold to us under the populist argument that if people spend all their lives paying tax, then why should they also pay it when they die? The issue is that low inheritance tax leads to the perpetuation of inequality of wealth down the generations. There is a reason why taxes like inheritance tax exist and were introduced.

You can see how this law is the most recent example of attempts to remove all property gains from taxation by the establishment political parties. To seek to remove all property worth a certain amount of money from inheritance tax is a way of putting a floor underneath house prices.

Is it right that we are moving towards an economic system where our generation is forced to wait until a relative dies, so that we can inherit a lump sum, before we can afford to buy a house of the kind that we grew up in? This is the system that many Conservatives want us to adopt. They want us to keep and accept the economic model of sky-high Land and House prices, regardless of the social divisions and inequality of wealth it causes.

PERCEPTION OF PROPERTY AS A SCARCE ASSET

This is more of a psychological phenomenon that is derived from the restricted supply of building Land. What I am talking here is a human social response to a scarce resource. When we perceive that a resource or an asset is scarce, our natural instinct is to *Horde* that resource. And so we are hordeing property. Well-off people with spare money tend to put it into property investments, whether they are families of buy-to-let investors.

This perception forms through widespread knowledge that houses are not being built in enough numbers, meaning that supply cannot keep up with demand. And so people realise that house prices will go up. And so this perception creates a further rush in demand to buy the commodity or asset (houses) that is perceived to be in shortage. And thus there is further upward pressure on house prices.

This psychological and human social phenomenon is ultimately caused by the Planning Law rigging the supply of Building Land. it's an important concept for you to understand, that the Planning Law has caused major changes in human social behaviour and the hoarding of property.

The scarcity of a resource or asset also causes intense human competition for that resource or asset. So people are competing with each other to buy property. And in London this competition has very intense in places, where houses have often been bid over their asking price, and also the act of Gazumping.

THE 'HELP TO BUY' SCHEME

A couple of years ago, in response to the housing crisis of affordability, the government introduced its 'Help to Buy' scheme. This is a scheme which has as its stated aim, to encourage more first time buyers to buy property that they otherwise would not be able to afford. It does this by offering you good savings rates on ISAs to encourage you to save up for a 5% deposit for your first home; and then provides you with a mortgage loan to make up for the remaining deposit of 25% you were not able to save up, to enable you to buy your first home.

The effect of this is to artificially increase demand for homes, demand that ordinarily would not exist because the people this is 'helping' would not be able to afford to buy a house. This is because house prices are so high that the deposit that the banks are demanding is not attainable by first time buyers, and many of our generation balk at taking on that level of debt.

All the Help to Buy policy has done is artificially stimulate Demand in the Housing Market. The Government has effectively subsidised the Housing Market at already high levels, thus further attempting to guarantee ever-rising house prices. It is Criminal that the Government is positively encouraging our generation to buy into high prices and getting us into eye-watering levels of debt. Given that house prices are already incredibly high, and the effective deposit is only 5%, it will take years before the owner starts to build up equity to pay back the government's equity loan. And after that they will still have the remaining 75% of the rest of the mortgage to pay back. By getting us to buy into already criminally high house prices, we will be buying an asset that is highly unlikely to increase much more in value over the time it takes to pay off the mortgage. So the owner may not even make enough on the future sale of the house to recover the interest costs on their mortgage. And, if the housing bubble bursts, they will lose all their equity too. At that point it really is slavery for these poor youngsters from our generation who bought these houses.

CHAPTER 4
SUMMARY & ARGUMENT

Over the past few chapters I have laid out the main factors and laws that affect house prices in this country. It should by now be quite apparent that Government law-making, whether deliberately or by accident' has accumulated a whole selection of laws and policies, that has resulted in the housing market being quite broken and house prices being the highest they have ever been relative to wages. To summarise this information, I have brought together information from different graphs together to give you an overall picture of what has happened in our housing market over the last 70 years. Below I also give you a timeline of the laws that have affected the housing market over the last 70 years. This will enable you to see the direct effect that these laws have had on house prices.

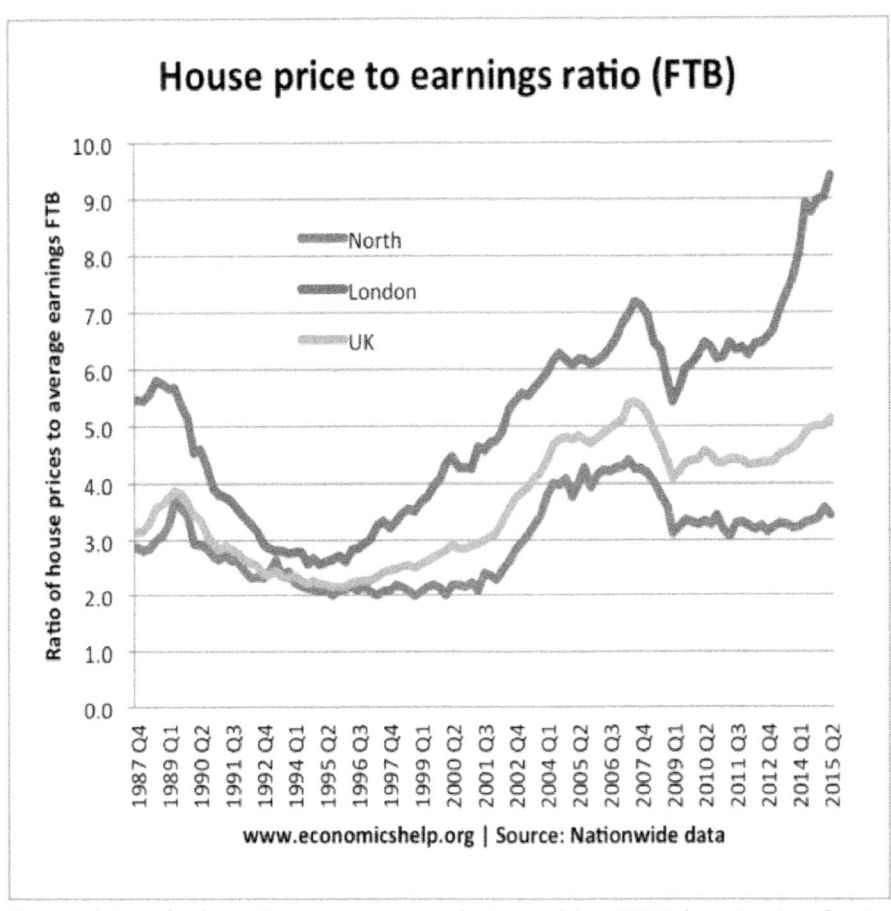

Original Article: http://www.economicshelp.org/blog/5709/housing/market/

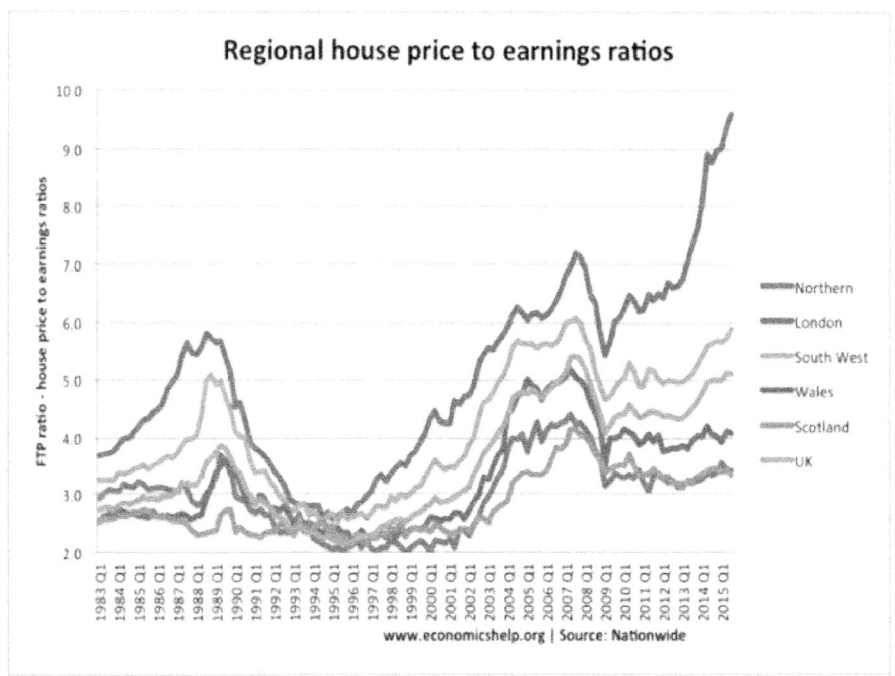

Reproduced by kind permission of economicshelp.org
Original Article: http://www.economicshelp.org/blog/5709/housing/market/

HOUSING AFFORDABILITY DATA

Region / Country	Average House Price (Current)	12 Month Change (%)	Average Annual Wage	House Price to Wage Ratio
Wales	£144,828	4%	£24,617	6
Scotland	£143,711	3%	£27,404	5
United Kingdom	£216,750	8%	£27,440	8
England	£232,885	9%	£26,884	9
London	£484,716	12%	£34,320	14

Reproduced by kind permission of Moneywise.co.uk
Original article: http://www.moneywise.co.uk/news/2016-10-12/uk-house-

prices-eight-times-average-wage

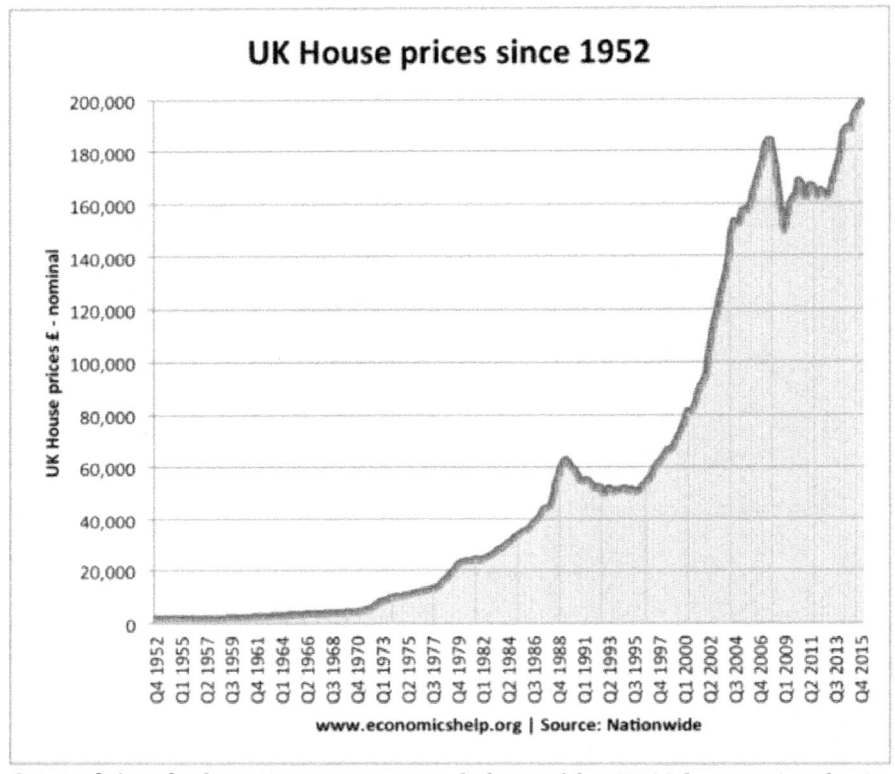

Original Article: http://www.economicshelp.org/blog/5709/housing/market/

Figure 4.2 Housing Completions, UK, 1950-2010

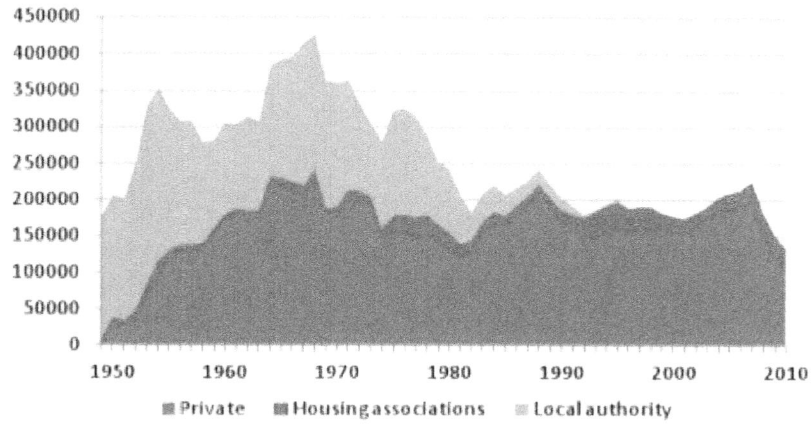

■ Private   ■ Housing associations   ■ Local authority

Source: Housing Completions, 1950-2010, CLG.

Original Article: http://www.economicshelp.org/blog/5709/housing/market/

I stated earlier that when Government nationalises the right to Build, it creates an obligation for itself to provide supply that the private sector finds it more difficult to do. You can see from this graph that since the early 1980s this obligation by Local Authorities has not been fulfilled. Government no longer builds the houses it is supposed to. So why is our Right to Build still nationalised if the Government is no longer willing to fulfill its obligations? We clearly should be doing this ourselves if Government won't.

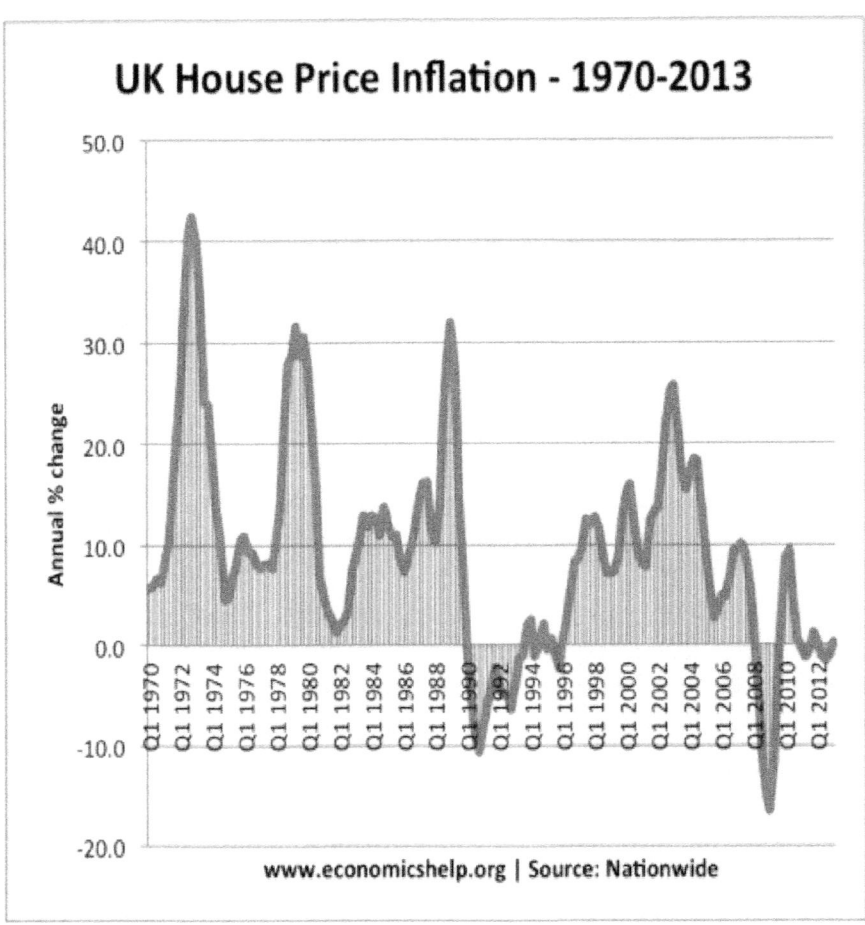

Original Article: http://www.economicshelp.org/blog/5709/housing/market/
On the left of the graph you can see the 40% house price rise that the Heath-Barber Boom caused in 1972, which was followed by a horrible inflationary crisis. It is also clear that there has been a downward trend in house price rises since the 1970s. The rise in prices since 2012 is not shown on this graph, but it has been no more than 10% per year, so the longer term downtrend is intact.

And last but by no means least, no data on the housing market would be complete without a graph showing interest rates:

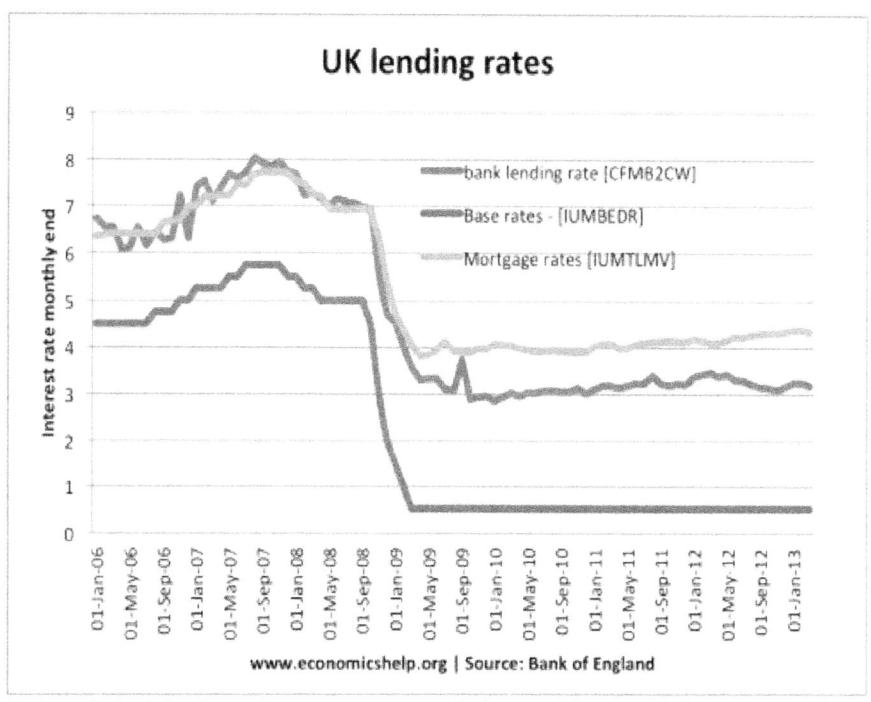

Original Article: http://www.economicshelp.org/blog/5709/housing/market/

Do not try to tell me that falling interest rates have not had a huge impact on house prices! This doesn't even take account of the recent fall in rates.

The information above and the book content so far should start to make it clear to you what has been going on in our society the past 70 years. But in case it isn't, and also to hammer the point home to you, I am proudly going to list, in order, the changes in law and policies, that have led us to the perpetual housing crisis that we are now in, together with the political party that carried them out. Ha!

1947 - Labour Government introduces the First Planning Act, that Nationalises the right to build on Land, resulting in government having the obligation to ensure that housing supply is sufficient for the country's needs. Building Land prices start to rise dramatically.

1949 - Labour Government passes the National Parks and Access to the Countryside Act 1949 that introduces the concept of Areas of Outstanding

Natural Beauty.

1954 - Tory Government updates the Planning Law updated via the 1954 Planning Act.

1955 - Tory Government issues the Greenbelt Circular, which encircles major towns and cities with a ring of Land that cannot be built on. There was no vote in Parliament to pass this. Building Land prices begin to rise even more dramatically.

1972 - Tory Chancellor Anthony Barber liberalises the Banking system and credit, leading to the 'Heath-Barber Boom', where Houses Prices increased 40% in 1 year. Leads to Stagflation, industrial unrest and 3-day week.

1990 - Tory Government passes the Town and Country Planning Act 1990 which consolidates all Land and Planning Law into one Act. This includes the Greenbelt Circulars which previously had not been voted on.

1997 - Tony Blair's Labour Government hands control over interest rates to Bank of England, which immediately lowers interest rates several times, starting the house price boom we have seen over the last 20 years.

2008 - Labour Government passes the Planning Act 2008.

2008 - Bank of England lowers interest rates to the lowest they have ever been, in response to the Financial Crisis. It also starts Quantitative Easing, causing house prices to recover quickly and then surge to new highs over the following 9 years.

2011 - Tory-Liberal Coalition Government passes the Localism Act 2011.

2016 - UK votes to leave the EU.

2017 - Tory Government issues it Housing 'White Paper', that contains no reforms. House prices are the highest they have ever been.

What can we learn from all this Firstly, we can all now see how a succession of laws and policies has accompanied the obscene house price rises we have seen over the last 70 years.

And you can also see that all the main players of the Political-Economic Establishment Elite have contributed to this. Labour, The Tories, The Bank of England, Liberal Democrats. They have all played their part.

And because there have been so many of these law changes, one after the other over 70 years, it therefore follows that these laws are all responsible for the rises in house prices. It is no coincidence. And if all our laws come from Deliberate Human Action, as they surely do, then House Prices and the Housing Crisis has been caused by Deliberate Human Action.

So Deliberate Human Action has restricted the supply of building Land and therefore houses in our country.

My view is that the Planning Law was originally brought in by Labour because of their desire to Command and Control as much of the economy as possible. Part of this involved Nationalising the right to develop Land and making us all have to ask for permission. And then when the Tories saw what it was doing to Land and property prices in the 1950s, they starting augmenting the law and restricting supply further with the introduction of new laws, so that their own interests were served. A few decades after that we have seen the tampering with Demand via beneficial tax law, offshore tax havens arising, etc. This all adds together to create the perfect environment for ever-rising house prices, up to a point.

We can see that comparatively little of the rise in house prices has been down to general inflation in the economy. If that was the case, the price of a Chicken would be £51 now. It isn't, it's still under £10. And you can eat a Whole Chicken in Nandos for £13 by the way. And Milk would set you back a Tenner. That is how Criminally Obscene House Prices are in our country.

In the next edition of this book I will show this timeline as part of a grand graph of house prices, in order for you to see the impact in pictorial form. Unfortunately I did not have the time to prepare it for this first edition.

THE CORN LAWS

Before I go on I want to tell you about an occasion in our country's history when we had to endure a Rigged Market for many decades. This extract from Wikipedia is a good summary:

The **Corn Laws** were measures enforced in the United Kingdom between 1815 and 1846, which imposed restrictions and tariffs on imported grain. They were designed to keep grain prices high to favour domestic producers. The laws did indeed raise food prices and became the focus of opposition from urban groups who had far less political power than rural Britain. The Corn Laws imposed steep import duties, making it too expensive to import grain from abroad, even when food supplies were short. The laws were supported by Conservative Landowners and opposed by Whig industrialists and workers. The Anti-Corn Law League was responsible for turning public and elite opinion against the laws, in a large, nationwide middle-class moral crusade with a Utopian vision. We need to do the same with the Housing Market.

While I will not delve too deeply into the reasons the laws were imposed in the first place, the long term consequences and effects on food prices are what i am concerned with. Suffice to say that over many decades they rigged the price of basic foodstuffs that contributed to widespread famines killing large numbers of people.

The Corn Laws enhanced the profits and political power associated with Land ownership. Their abolition saw a significant increase of free trade.

The reason I am mentioning the Corn Laws in this book is because are an example of market Rigging that has occurred in this country in the past. It is relevant to the current situation . It tookdecades and the creation of the Anti-Corn Law movement before Parliamentfinally repealed the Corn Laws. So many of them dragged their feet for solong on the matter that when the vote to repeal was finally won, it still was
only won by a relatively slim margin.

https://en.wikipedia.org/wiki/Corn_Laws

What is the Definition of a Rigged Market? According the Cambridge English Dictionary, it is "**The practice of unfairly or illegally controlling the sale or the price of Products, Commodities or Assets, etc**". I replaced the original word 'Shares' with Assets and added in Commodities because of their relevance to the global marketplace and price rigging. Now let's relate this to the Housing Market. Let's go through the key words in this sentence that are used to form the definition of a Rigged Market. Houses are an **Asset**, yes? Of course they are, they meet the criteria of something that gives

'Rights or Other Access to Future Economic Benefits as a Result of a Past Transaction or Event' to give you a technical Finance wording. In other words they can generate an income and profit. And is the price of Houses **Controlled**? I would say so, because the Planning Law severely controls what can and can't be done with Land and Property without permission - and as it controls the supply of Building Land and therefore Houses, logically the price of Houses is also controlled. Has this been done **Unfairly** or **Illegally**? Not technically Illegally as Parliament had the right to pass these laws in our country, they are our elected lawmakers after all. How about Unfairly? We can gauge the unfairness of the Housing Market by which socio-demographics may be Unfairly affected. Ok, it's pretty obvious the Housing Market is grossly Unfair as most of an entire generation are either locked out of the Housing Market or can only afford a Hovel, even the very successful ones, and they are debt slaves. So, we can see that the Housing Market meets most of the key-word criteria of Cambridge University's definition of a Rigged Market.

Quite a punchy title isn't it? One of my goals for 2017 is to persuade as many people as possible to use the phrase Rigged Housing Market when talking about the Housing Market in general.

The Government recently came out and admitted that the Housing Market was broken in our country. That in itself is surprising for them to admit it, as it's a step in the right direction. But it's a bit more that that isn't it, Parliament? . They'vebeen deliberately Rigging it for decades because they want House Prices tokeep on rising forever. At least 80% of Land in this country has a ban onbuilding on it - that's why houses are not getting built - the bureaucracy andprocess is secondary to this Fundamental Fact.

The inherent bias in our laws is all about restricting supply, inhibiting supply wherever possible, and artificially boosting demand. It's been like that for 70 years. Because they want prices to rise. They have wanted to make economic serfs of us. That's been the whole point.

The UK housing market with all its laws, is actually the most tampered-with and controlled market in the world. For all this time, all along, the wool has been pulled over our eyes. Law, after law, after law, has worked to push up Land and house prices to levels that are beyond ridiculous.

The reason that *you* cannot buy your first house, cannot afford to upsize, or are in wage-debt-slavery for most of the rest of your actual life is because successive governments have deliberately passed a succession of laws for 70 years that effectively rigs the housing market to the upside. They have artificially restricted supply, artificially boosted demand under the guise of 'helping people to get on the housing ladder'. The reality is that they pass these laws to push up house prices.

They have banned squatting in empty houses, but what have they done to stop the houses from being empty in the first place? Very little - higher council tax is all they get charged, and as long as 1 person is living in the house, they can get around that. Squatting is a natural economic solution to a housing shortage. It is natural human behaviour to make use of assets in a poor condition that are not being used for anything. And it is a symptom of a failing economic housing model based on a totalitarian planning system and a lack of tax. It is a natural cultural reaction to a poor use of economic resources and poor law-making. Many squatters, I suspect, are the types of people who would end up living communally in the countryside if they were able to.

This is the biggest misallocation of economic resources ever, forcing people to buy into exorbitant house prices, and is slavery or serfdom by the back (or front) door. Quite frankly, it looks clear to me that this property has been Rigged toward ever higher prices, to force us to buy into a housing market at high prices, to force us into a life of constant debt-slavery.

What I do know, is that the numerous laws that have led Supply of new Houses to be restricted, and the Demand of Houses to be boosted, are anything but an accident. All of this surely cannot be an accident. It is Rigged. The restrictions on Building Land have caused the proportion of Land cost of a new home to go up from 25% in the 1950s to over 70% now.

Buildings themselves have not really become any more valuable over the past few decades, when you take into account inflation in the rest of the economy. It is the Land they sit on that has soared in value, due to the Planning Law and so many other Laws, causing a Rigged Housing Market. It is the Land that houses sit on that is making House prices too high. And the Land market is Rigged.

In fact, if you start off with a restricted supply of an asset, then any attempts to make it easier for people to buy that asset merely stimulates demand even further, perpetuating the Rigged market even further.

I have shown to you how the various laws in the UK have conspired together to create a Rigged Market of ever-rising house prices and debt-slavery to some unseen force. It is just possible that it could be an accident of law, or incompetence of Parliament, but it is just as likely to be malicious intent. The only way out of this situation in the short term is a housing market crash or ruinous inflation, where everybody suffers except the big landowners. With the recent crash in the value of the pound on international markets, it seems more likely to be the 2nd option, but there is no sign of the wage inflation that would drive this. Is the real price of Brexit falling house prices and higher interest rates?

CHAPTER 5
DEBATE

So I have now argued that the Housing Market we all have to deal with in our country has been Rigged for 70 years, by a selection of Laws brought in since the end of the 2nd World War that seeks to maximise Building Land prices and thus House Prices. I'm not sorry to have to say that, but that is exactly what it looks like, especially when you compare the current situation to the Corn Laws in the 19th century.

Increasing numbers of us have felt in recent years that there is something fundamentally wrong and not quite right. It is not just that the Housing Market is broken. There may be something else going on that we feel uneasy about, but we do not quite know exactly what it is. But we now know that the property has been Rigged for too long now.

It's all Rigged. It's all a great, big con.

But *why* is it Rigged? To find out, we should take a look at who benefits from this situation. The older generations, yes, who managed to get into the market when house prices were lower relative to wages, and when inflation was higher, and so their debt would be eroded away relatively quickly by wage rises. The existing major Land-owners, such as the Aristocracy, who still own a third of the Land in this country. Certain members of the aristocracy own the best and most valuable parts of London.

Ask yourselves, why is it that in other countries around the world, citizens have the fundamental right to settle and build where they want? Because other western countries believe in these fundamental human rights. They recognise the fundamental right of people to settle and build their own home. It was part of the original American dream to be Free and to build your own home. Now compare that to the situation in the UK.

Don't you find it a bit strange that just as the 20th century was bringing the technological advances in construction techniques and material transportation that enabled housebuilding to be available to the masses almost anywhere in the countryside, that the government then brings in a slew of post-war laws designed to make it nearly impossible to achieve that?

Is this all supposed to be an accident of law-making? Was it an accident that successive governments over the course of 70 long years have passed a whole selection of laws, that have done little except to put long term real house prices on an ever-upward trend? If it is an accident, then our politicians must surely be the most inept and *incompetent* bunch of people this country has ever known. If it is not an accident, then our politicians are the most *corrupt* bunch of people of this country has ever known. Take your pick! Nowhere else in the world has this been allowed to happen. For a generation of people to be so completely disenfranchised from society, that not only does it look like a conspiracy, but it feels like one, and begins to look like a deliberate long term step in a game plan much more sinister. If this carries on, what is the end-point of this current situation? Why are we being wilfully pushed towards neo-serfdom?

It is the biggest con this country has ever known. It goes further than the Corn Laws. In the 21st century we have a system where almost half the Land in this country is still owned by the aristocracy and the government, and yet the cost of basic Shelter is the highest it's ever been relative to our wages. People need to open their eyes and see it for the con and Rigged Market that it is.

None of this ever gets said in the media in any depth. They don't actually say that the primary reason why house prices are so high is that there is an actually law that says that 80+ of the physical Land in this country has a ban on building on it. They don't say that the supply is so restricted that the housing market is a one-way game. They don't state the obvious truth of the matter. And no-one attacks the very concept of planning permission and the planning law. Because they are dumbed-down and part of the Establishment. Which shows quite clearly how the media is the tool of the Establishment Elite.

TO ENSERF A PEOPLE

So if you wanted to enserf a nation of people, while still giving the impression that they lived in a free and fair society, how would you do it? First, you need to understand what Serfdom is. Serfdom is the condition where the person is held in Bondage to another, higher authority, and is required to work, in order so that they be able to satisfy some basic condition of living. Like owning the roof over their heads. So if Serfdom is forcing somebody to work for you, how do you go about forcing somebody to perform labour for you? Well, a good way to do this while making them still think that they are free is to manipulate the price of the most expensive item they are likely to buy, and ideally have little choice to buy, by creating an ideology. If you create an ideology of owning that asset at the same time as rigging the market for it, so that the person feels compelled to buy it, because so many others are too. And the person, not being able to afford to buy it outright anyway will have to get a large loan to buy it. And if you rig the market for it so that the price of the asset is always going up, and therefore the mortgage the person needs to get to buy it is always large, and the monthly loan payments take a correspondingly large amount of the person's monthly wage… Well, you have bonded that person to you, and they feel compelled to keep working and acting in a way that is suitable to you. Now, what is the single biggest item of expenditure in our lives? A House. And has the price of it been Rigged? Yep. So it looks like we are Serfs already and have been for 70 years.

Take the physical representation of people's hopes, dreams and life's work, and ruthlessly set about Rigging the price of it, to make them work for decades longer than they need to. To force them to work for longer so that they may not lead the life they truly want to. That's not very nice, is it?

Please do not be too upset by all of this. There is a way out of this. The way of life in this country does not have to be this way. We can change this country and its illiberal, restrictive ways.

What I am saying here, is that once you are paying above a certain price for your Shelter, so that your mortgage is at such an extreme level, you are effectively having to work harder and for longer in order to pay off your 'debt' that is caused by a Rigged Land Price . This is not about Left vs Right. This is about
Liberalism vs Conservatism.

THE COUNTRYSIDE AND CONSERVATION

When you look at what the Land in this country is physically being used for, most of it is arguably used for extensive arable and animal farming. While we do need to have a certain self-sufficiency in food as a nation, continued extensive arable and animal farming (rather than intensive) is not the way forward. It takes up far too much space in a country that has a limited amount of space, and which desperately needs the space taken up by extensive farming for other uses. Arable farming, that is, the use of Land for growing plants for food or industrial use on an extensive scale, makes very little money per-acre and generates very little calories per acre compared to Animal Husbandry and Fruit Farming. I say that Arable farming takes up so much Land in our countryside, that it contributes to making Land scarce generally. It makes Land scarce for other uses, because it's being used for Arable farming. This is Land that could and should be used for other uses, such as Homes, Forests, Infrastructure and more intensive agriculture over a smaller area. Rapeseed, for example, is a non-food arable product that is grown in this country and then exported abroad to places like Egypt where it is made into Food Oil. A vast amount of Land is given over to growing Rapeseed, bringing a relatively small amount of money into this country, and yet we don't even eat the stuff! It is not food, and it is exported. It does not contribute to food security at all! This is an example of how the Land of our country, through the effect of multiple Laws and Policies, is effectively being misused on a mass scale. It is not being used for what Society needs it to be used for.

We protect the countryside for our own 'benefit', mainly. But what's the point of protecting the countryside if we, the people, cannot live in it or enjoy it because we can't build our own houses or buy one because the prices are too high? Even the people who live in the countryside are not allowed to build their own houses there. The degree of local government control is unbearable. By allowing them to control the situation we are subject to their petty local partisan politics and jealousies when they find someone who earns more than them.

The 'sacred' countryside is man-made. Thousands of years of ploughing has altered its appearance and its geographical layout irrevocably. And it changes naturally anyway. When police use old Landscape photos to help them search for missing dead bodies, they tend to find the Landscape today looks very different from what it used to in the old photo.

Conceptually and Physically, the Countryside is man-made anyway, so this idea of preserving the 'sacred countryside' because it is 'natural' is really smoke and mirrors to hide what is really going on. The Rigging of our very Way of Life. The Denial for us to be able to *settle* where we want. The deliberate trapping of us inside artifical planning boundaries. The deliberate forcing of us to pay much higher prices and spend much longer paying off our mortgages than is necessary. It has affected everyone. Think of all the choices you would have had in life to do all the things you truly wanted to do if you were able to pay off your mortgage sooner. Think about it. Our country just doesn't have to be like this. It's a great con to restrict the supply of building Land and keep prices going up forever. To keep us all in Bondage.

Historically, many prominent public figures have campaigned for 'saving the countryside'. Many of these people are very Rich and they own large estates. Conservationism has historically been very a fashionable movement for the Rich to adopt. When they get rich and buy their estates, they often become 'Lifestyle Farmers'. And because their money has bought their estate, they don't want anybody else to enjoy it or ruin their view. Oh, so it's perfectly alright for the Rich to pursue their fashionable policy of Conservationism in the name of conserving the Land and its supposedly natural habitat, but the cost of this is always on the other 99% of us who end up having to pay through the nose for the Land that our houses sit on, as a result of restricting where houses can be built due to 'Conservationism'.

As if the countryside is going to disappear because you start letting people build their own houses on it. For that to happen you would need a population of about 500 million+ people in this country who explicitly decide to all spread out over the entire country. And it just will not happen.

If we let people build on the countryside, it's not going to disappear tomorrow. *Or Ever.* You would need a billion people to come and settle here before that happened. It's a fallacy to say that 'We have to stop all building on the countryside in order to save it and keep it'. It's Rubbish. It's Bullshit.

MARX AND THE COMMUNIST MANIFESTO

Marxism was really just a way and a theory for dealing with the perceived problems associated with a particular type of economic model in the 19th century. If Marx were alive today, the communist manifesto would look a lot different and it would be fundamentally changed to suit the particular economic crisis of our time, the Housing Crisis. His manifesto would seek to solve the problems in the housing market, in the particular way that suited his own personal beliefs and aims, rather than what would be best for the people of this country.

Marx and Engels took a balloon ride over London to picture and describe the issues of the 19th century. These days we can just look on Google Earth!

Where Marx uses the term 'Class Struggle', I prefer the term 'Tribal Evolution'. As the economy develops over several hundred years in a society, wealth periodically becomes concentrated in fewer pairs of hands, and is then periodically redistributed either to a different set of hands or downward to the 99%. The whole process is essentially 'pushing the reset button' before the cycle starts again. It happens in order for the tribe to survive, because if it doesn't happen another stronger tribe will come along and take us over. There are plenty of examples of this throughout English and British history. I do not see the development of Indo-European societies over many thousands of years in the context of 'Class Struggle'. It is a process of periodic reform and adaptation in order to be able to survive as a society, as a tribe. Indo-european civilisation has been so successful since around 4000 bc because it is able to innovate and market (use & sell) those innovations. Germanic civilisation has done the same. And the Normans did the same too. Those tribes that can innovate and market those innovations across the tribe, will dominate and out-survive those tribes that do not. Communism has not survived because it does not innovate and market. Liberal Centre-Right society has been able to survive so far because it had an inherent capability built into it that allows society to innovate and market, and so it remains useful as a political-economic model.

Marx's idea of nationalising the means of production for the benefit of the proletariat was unsustainable, and all countries who have tried to do it have failed. Where it has been adopted it has led to industrial decline and curtailed innovation and productivity, some of the main drivers of economic growth.

Honestly, I think the Left versus Right debate that Jeremy Corbyn's Labour Party are trying to force on us, is a distraction and is out-of-date in many ways. I think that the real debate for the young is about creativity and liberalism versus a lifetime of debt-slavery. Labour do not have much interest at all in Liberty. They seek to consolidate the wealth of the nation into the hands of the State, which in many ways is the same outcome of the Central-Banker Financial Capitalism we have seen in recent times. They want to control our lives, and too many of them have destructive personalities, not creative personalities. Yes, the inequality of wealth is the worst it has ever been. Class division in this country appears to be among the worst it has ever been. But I argue that this has mainly been caused by political stagnation, the status quo of the globalisation movement, but most of all, the Illiberal Rigged Housing Market for the past 70 years. The ever-rising house prices and the link to debt-slavery that the mortgage market has perpetuated. Even if you manage to buy a house and then succeed in paying off your debt-slavery, it's highly unlikely you will ever be able to retire and so you will be forever locked into a life of labour until the day you die. The older generation who are still working are being screwed over on their pensions to such an extent that they will never have enough money for retirement.

The fact is that the Left have no good solution for the housing crisis that doesn't risk more state control over our already over-controlled housing market. All they will seek to do is build more council houses and try to get most of the young generation to live in their council houses, as part of fulfilling their communist utopian ideal that is unachievable.

People are perfectly willing to go on accepting Capitalism, so long as they are given the opportunity to achieve major life goals without submitting themselves to debt-slavery. They want the option to build their own house and are not forced to submit to some major form of control in their lives. Free Will and Determination.

But if we do not soon get the Land and Property Supply and Tax Side reform that we need in our society, for our society to be able to survive over the long term... *Then we may need to push that 'Reset Button'.*

THE EUROPEAN WAY OF LIFE

Our European way of life has its roots in bronze age tribes that are referred to today as the indo-europeans. These were a collection of tribes who became semi-nomadic through pastoralism, horse-riding, and wagon-use. This resulted in them wandering far and wide from their original homes in Southern Russia/Ukraine, to populate and dominate mainLand Europe.

LIBERALISM

The fundamental way our society has always worked, is that you can do pretty much whatever you want here, so long as there is not a law saying you can't. In other words, the default setting is that you can do what you want, not 'you have to ask permission before you do anything'. So why is the housing market so illiberal? Why do we have to ask for permission to Create?

We claim to live in a Liberal society that values Freedom, and we have (allegedly) fought wars over this concept, most notably World War 2. So if we fought so long and hard during WW2 and so many people lost their lives and their loved ones, in order so that we would supposedly have our Freedom, then why within a few years of its end did the government embark on a slew of Land and Property laws that over 70 years, the lifetime of communism, has enslaved us with the mortgages on an ever-rising housing market that we are told we must buy into? Why did we bother to fight Nazism and Fascism if, after we win, we then allowed ourselves to be subjected to a lifetime of debt-slavery? In a Rigged Housing Market? When it just *is not necessary*?

How can we claim to live in a Liberal Democracy and a Free-Market Society when the price of the Land that we are sitting on right now, has been Rigged, quite literally by the Law of the Land?

I say that the restrictive laws on house building are so Illiberal compared to the rest of the world, that they constitute a violation of our Fundamental Human Rights.

Is it right that the price of basic Shelter is beyond all reason? We ban building on 90% of the Land in this country, in the name of what?

What Fundamental Human Rights am I talking about in the context of this book? What is this Liberalism? Should we define Liberalism and Human Rights as the Freedom for people to behave in a natural way, to follow what comes naturally to mankind? If this is the case then surely the Freedom to Roam and to *Settle* where we want to comes near to the top of the list. I argue that there should be a fundamental set of Freedoms for the British people, and one of those Freedoms must be the Freedom to settle and live where you want in this country. Virtually anywhere. Regardless of whether it's in a national park, or so-called 'protected' areas etc.

Fundamentally, what is it that people want in their lives, in this country? We want to be able to do what we want, when we want, how we want to. It is the Freedom to work as hard or as little as they like, to benefit economically from the fruits of their labour, to keep most of the fruits of their labour, and to reasonably live how they please, so long as the rights of others are not infringed. They want to have a secure and safe Shelter, a place to live, at a good price. Most people in this country want to *Create*, in a way that is acceptable to them. They want to *Create* a life for themselves, or *Create* children, or *Create* a Home for themselves. When someone wants to start a business, that is usually but not always an expression of the will to Create something, to Build something. When it boils down to it, when people want to have Freedom and Liberty in their lives, what they are saying is they want the Freedom to *Create and Experience.* One of the main points I have been trying to make in this book is that the British people do not currently have the Freedom to Create in one of the fundamental ways that humanity wants to express its Creativity. To Create a Home for themselves.

If we ask ourselves the question: How do we want to live our lives? What do we want to do, on a holistic level? One of the answers to this is the very European need to Roam, to at times lead a semi-nomadic lifestyle, and to eventually Settle. This is one of the basic dreams that European people have, and have always had. To have a Base from which you can carry on roaming, but can always eventually come back to. Whether it's a daily commute as part of your job, or time out travelling, we all want the safety and security of a permanent base to come back to. Whether you are an individual, a family, a commune of friends even, a religious group, or a retiree, we want to have our permanent base from which to Roam and Explore. To deny this right for so long to the very people you represent as a politician is a gross violation of the European way of life, of Human Rights, of our Way. It is repressive, and deserves to be swept away.

Now Ask yourselves: In Life, What is the major achievement that you would like to to be able to work towards, that the law, because it is so unreasonable and illiberal, does not let you do? What is one of the dreams that most of us have in common that could reasonably be achievable in our lifetimes? I suspect the answer may be to build to your own Home, where you want to. The desire to Create a Home for ourselves is something that most of us have in common.

Philosophically, What Is The Land There For? It is there for our use. The bottom line is that the countryside is there for our use as we are the dominant species on this planet. But how can conservationists claim that you cannot build on the countryside at all, because it needs to be protected, when the current condition of the countryside is not even environmentally friendly with arable farming and the lack of trees.

This is about Liberalising the most Illiberal part of the British way of life.

Liberal thought and politics in this country has recently been more concerned with railing against the so-called 'Nanny State', but in reality most of the laws that liberals and libertarians attack are really designed to protect us from those of us who seek to exploit for their own immoral gain. The ban on smoking in public places, speed limits, the ban on using mobile phones in cars - these are health and safety measures more than anything else. These are comparatively minor liberal issues. They are a distraction from the major liberal issues that our society actually faces. What I am showing you is that there are much bigger issues of Liberty that our society silently faces, and that these are now causing major dislocation in society.

David Lloyd George, the Liberal Prime Minister who introduced the first budget aimed at Liberal redistribution of wealth, taxed increases in Land Values for the first time. He rightly saw that it was Land and development of Land and the failure to tax the gains on Land, that led to inequality of wealth, so he taxed it, in order to redistribute it. But within 3 years of Lloyd George's death on 23 March 1945, the 1947 Planning Act was proposed which Rigged the Housing Market. Less than 4 years later, on 1 July 1948, it became Law. Is it a coincidence that within 4 years of Lloyd George's death you saw the introduction of a Planning law that successive Governments have been able to manipulate to Rig the price of basic Shelter over 70 years?

If David Lloyd George were alive again today, 100 years after he first was, was active in the 21st century rather than the early 20th century, then he would probably immediately recognise the same problems today that existed in the early 20th century. That the huge inequality of wealth has been caused by an Elite that finds it too easy to Avoid and Evade paying tax. That a large part of the inequality stems from the housing market divide. That our society is still plagued by the same old problems that existed before. And he would waste no time in setting about taxing the gains on Land property again, at source like I will propose.

Liberalising the housing market and rolling back the planning law will not harm any other person, unlike Smoking in public places or de-restricting Gun law. It most definitely *will* create huge potential for economic growth...

THE ECONOMY

What are 'Property Rights'? Property rights are usually expressed in terms of economics, that is, how the thing we own is used. Typically Property Rights mean we can use the Thing, earn income from the Thing, Sell or Transfer the Thing to others, and to enforce your Rights to the Thing, the right to Keep the Thing. This is all very well and good, but it contains an assumption - that we already own the Thing, and that we were reasonably able to come into possession of the Thing. Property Rights say nothing about the right to be able to acquire the Thing in the first place. And this is a point I want to emphasise. That the Housing market is so illiberal in this country that the assumption that there is a reasonable chance that people will be able to acquire a property is no longer valid. That the market is so Rigged that the young cannot own meaningful Property, therefore that essentially there are minimal property rights for the young because of the high barrier to entry. The Young do not currently have a meaningful Right to acquire Property because of its unattainability. I have shown that Property Rights by themselves are not good enough for our society as they currently stand. The state of our housing market shows that the Right to Acquire Property Rights needs to be a written as a fundamental human right to *acquire at a reasonable price*. And that it needs to be enforced. Given that the government is responsible for Rigging the Housing Market through the laws it has enacted over 70 years, it can only be right that government plays a leading role in de-rigging the housing market, that is, by liberalising it. The government already facilitates the right to acquire property by people who otherwise would not be able to do so. An example of this is enabling council house tenants to buy their council houses, at a price that is affordable. So, why not do the same with Land that has development rights attached, to enable the British people to build their own homes on Land that was previously owned by the government? This is common sense and pragmatism.

https://en.wikipedia.org/wiki/Town_and_Country_Planning_Act_1947

I have again shown the link for the first post-war planning act. Note the

Wikipedia sentence 'Ownership of the Land does not automatically confer the right to build on it'. This is in full view of the public, and is making the point that this is a blatant infringement of fundamental property rights, that is the right to do with your Land as you please. Just what is wrong with building a house in the middle of the countryside? We would like to do it. So why won't they let us, seeing as the countryside will not disappear?

So what does all this mean, when the younger generation has a lack of property rights because of their inability to acquire property in the first place, because of the barriers to entry to ownership.. And what is the result of this for our society over the long-term? Our generation is turning away from participation in society and thewider economy.

I can understand why so many of our generation are turning their backs on home-ownership. By not getting into debt, you maintain a degree of Freedom. Real Freedom is financial Freedom, and the choices it affords you. Being financially free is not just only about being rich. It can also be about *not being in debt*. It is about avoiding the wage-debt serfdom that the Establishment Elite in this country expects our generation to submit to, just so that they can cash in on and realise the gains they their generation has made on their housing obsession, and sustain ever-rising house prices.

There are Implications for future business and economic growth of this country if the young are not empowered to acquire and build up wealth.

Conventional economic theory says that the Land and Resources should reside in the hands of those who can make the best use out of them. If the Land should reside in the hands of those who can use it best, according to economic theory, then why are Land prices so high that they constitute an extreme barrier to entry to those who know best what to do with it? I don't just mean businesses and potential entrepreneurs. I mean people like us, who are tomorrow's business people, who might also like to build their own homes.

The Land owned by all the Landowners in our country almost never finds its way onto the open market to get sold. This has the effect of locking up the

Land market in the UK. The reason it doesn't find its way onto the open market is because of 2 main reasons. Firstly, the Planning Law means Landowners cannot do anything to develop their Land, meaning they are not motivated to sell it; and Secondly, the EU money that Landowners receive encourages them to hold onto the Land.

The failure to tax Land and buildings properly means that large amounts of brownfield Land, derelict buildings, etc, are just left to go to rack and ruin because the owners are not taxed or penalised into actually doing something with the Land. And so they hold onto it year after year, knowing that they can do so and get away with it.

I have already said that the Agricultural Land in our country is basically misused by Landowners. Part of the reason for this, on top of the Planning Law and the EU CAP, is the way Land is taxed too. There is no annual Land tax applied to Landowners. The ideal system is probably a compromise of the 2 different methods, a per-acre Annual Land Tax, and the Income or Corporation Tax that is paid based on Land activity of sorts. An Annual Land Tax will ensure that people are motivated to actually do something with the Land they own. The revenue raised from this can go towards funding a lower rate of Corporation Tax, something that the Government is already proposing in the wake of Brexit to make our economy more competitive. Thus a low Corporation Tax rate combined with an Annual Land Tax will ensure that Land starts to be put to the best, most economic use.

One of the biggest issues with the way our housing market works is the principle of 'Caveat Emptor'. This is the principle of 'buyer beware', and it is the concept of 'it's up to the buyer to do their homework and research on the property they are buying, rather than the seller having to inform the buyer of the various issues that need to fixed. This is really just a way for sellers to con unwary buyers into paying a higher price for a property than they otherwise should have done. I argue that 'caveat emptor', really just results in unwary people paying over the odds for properties that ought to have been priced a lot less because of the all the problems associated with them that need fixing. Again, this has to stop. When such a large amount of money is being paid for assets, and is likely to be the biggest purchase we make in our lives, then there should be a moral and legal onus on the current owner to provide information on these weaknesses and adjust the price. I justify this by saying that it is the Seller, because they own the property and therefore have the experience through living in it, of being in the strongest position to know about all the issues with it, all the maintenance that needs performing, and the likely costs involved, who should be charged with providing this information, and that the default position of the law should be that the seller is liable. Is it right that the seller can know about all these details, and then deliberately and irresponsibly not tell the buyer, while setting an asking price that does not take into account the costs that put it right? Too many people have been conned out of a lot of money, because the law lets them, and very few building surveys pick up these issues.

The rapidly rising house pricesthat the new planning laws created, would have seeped through to the widereconomy, causing prices of all goods and services to go up. Propertyinflation spread to the rest of the economy. This was not so damaging backthen, because there wasn't really the pensions industry that there is today, andpeople were more reliant on family and the state pension funded by taxes tofund their retirements, so their pension incomes were not really eroded byinflation. But if the government tries it today, they will get a big backlashfrom the hordes of retirees who typically vote Tory. The Tory party relies onthe votes of the middle-aged and the elderly to get elected, because thesepeople are the most likely to go out and vote. If these people feel out ofpocket, they will not vote in future elections. This effect will be amplified bythe aging population.

The Government has made a big thing about building 'Affordable Housing' over the last 10 years. But 'Affordable Housing' is a misnomer. This is because the biggest constituent of the cost of a new house is the cost of the Land it is sat on. And because the government has done nothing about reducing the cost of Building Land, the only way the cost of Land is reduced is by building smaller and smaller houses, which is exactly has been happening over the last 40 years anyway. So affordable housing is a fallacy, it does not exist at present, and will not exist until we free up the supply of Building Land.

The only way you can make the cost of a house affordable is by lowering the cost of the Land it is built on. Because that's the biggest portion of the price of the overall house. It's got nothing to do with the cost of building the house, or, in the long-term, the speed at which your house gets built. It is the cost of the Land, the supply of which is being restricted by the existence of artificial planning boundaries around each and every settlement in our country. So if you want the price of building Land to come down, you need to increase the supply of it. And the obvious and most direct way of doing that is by relaxing or abolishing the planning boundaries for people to build on.

The housebuilders clearly are not up the job of building houses that people actually want to live in, at affordable prices. People want to have the Freedom to decide where they live. People want to be able to live in the countryside and in the cities, if they choose to. Some people want to be town-dwellers. They do not want to be forced to live in mono-cultural suburban houses or blocks of flats. These are not, in my view, the kinds of places we should be bringing our children up in.

I will explain to you how the big housebuilders will not solve the housing crisis over the long run. The Government can say all it likes about how lots of houses are now being built, etc etc, but all of these so-called affordable homes can only be sold to us at outrageously high prices, otherwise the housebuilders will lose money. And this is because the housebuilders have had to pay very high prices for the Land that they build these houses on, meaning their costs are so high that their selling prices have to be high too. And if they cannot sell these houses at a profit in the short term, then they become financially weakened or go bust, meaning still less housebuilding in the long term, less supply and even higher residential and prices for existing residential areas, which building Land is valued with reference to. And this is due to the housing market being so fundamentally broken, because of the Planning Laws. If you have a Planning Law which bans building on 80%+ of the available Land in the country, for no justifiable reason, then any attempts to increase supply or stimulate demand without reforming that planning law will just result in economic damage, in the form of even higher Land prices or losses on new-build homes when supply is attempted to be increased, ruining house-builders. So you can see how the government's drive to build more houses in the short term and the long term just will not work without real Land and Property reform in this country. And this is because the supply of potential building Land is artificially restricted, this notion that you are not allowed to build houses in the so-called 'countryside'. Underlying all the issues in our housing market is the Planning Law which artificially restricts the amount of potential building Land by up to 80%+.

There is no competition among Landowners to sell Land. The reason for this is because they cannot develop their Land, to create the greatest economic value from it, and so they have no motivation to sell it. Especially if they are being paid CAP payments by the government. If all Landowners were able to develop, the right to develop was no longer nationalised, then they would start to *compete* with each other to sell or develop some of their Land, bringing down Building Land prices. And in turn this would begin to encourage a huge amount of housebuilding as building Land once more becomes affordable.

The Tory government has deliberately presided over rising house prices for decades since WW2. They have always wanted to push up house prices, as they see it as a good thing.

The Tories are desperately continuing to pass laws to let their generation selfishly lock in the gains they have made in the housing market. They are more obsessed with property than Labour was. The way they are passing law, they want to continue to bring property gains out of taxation altogether. They are desperately trying to misallocate more and more economic resources into forcing higher house prices, while getting away with building the fewest houses possible. There is lots of talk about building houses and setting targets, but very little real action and reform required to actually let it happen.

I saw an article in the Daily Telegraph proposing a cut in stamp duty. Again, this is an Establishment Elite attempt to encourage higher house prices. It will be dressed up as 'making it easier for first time buyers to buy their first house'. But stamp duty is already very low for the kinds of house that first time buyers want to buy i.e. up to a few hundred thousand pounds. The actual benefit will be to make it easier to buy more expensive property and for rich people to speculate and flip houses for short term gain. They also want to abolish capital gains tax, making it tax-free for the rich to speculate in the price of houses. These are all tax breaks that will just encourage higher house prices, that only the richest can afford. *Again, they are trying to rig the market even further, they are trying to push house prices up as far as possible.* This has to stop.

If the supply of building Land is increased by rolling back or eliminating the planning boundaries, in totality or for certain sections of the population, then the tax revenue associated with the Landowner selling all that extra Land for housebuilding is going to up. Alot. This is classic supply-side reform bringing in benefits for the government as well as the people. If building Land prices fall as a result of the increased supply of building Land, then the sheer extra quantity of building Land being sold to us will bring much more tax revenue to the taxman than the current highly restricted system does. So reform will benefit everyone, even the government.

THE SOCIAL IMPACT

There are secondaryimpacts on the social behaviour of those who cannot buy in, and thedownstream impacts on those throughout the rest of society. Too manypeople in my age bracket have turned their backs on ever owning a home, andhave sought solace in left-wing politics. Some people have turned to outrightcriminality, or refuse to pay taxes. Some refuse to get married. Others refuseto buy into what they know will be a lifetime of debt. Some young womenmove into the sex industry as a second job to earn enough money to save fora property or pay off their University debt. Some men go into drug dealing tomake enough to save for a house or pay off their debts.

The quality of life in the cities and countryside is little changed from 100 years ago.

The living conditions faced by many today are little better, and relative to today's upper classes, the same, as the infamous city slums in Britain of the early 20th century. Whole families, not just young couples, are living in 1-room flats/dwellings. I argue that these slums have never really disappeared: But the people who lived in them did, when they were killed off in their droves by being sent off to die in 2 World Wars or bombed during the Blitz.

It is government policy and law-making that has created the current situation that we are in, so it should be government who is responsible for fixing this mess. I do not propose that millions of government-owned council houses are built. This is the domain of the Left Wing, and does not work, as well as making society more dependent on the state. Too often the estates that these houses are built in become slums. And the government cannot be trusted to build large quantities of houses in an efficient way, whether they contract out to building companies or not. Instead I propose that the government sell off some of the vast amounts of Land that it owns, to us, the people, for people to build their own houses on.

If there is ever some kind of 'revolution', its cause will be rooted in the extreme dissatisfaction and disenfranchisement of the current under-40s generation. It will not be because of 'Brexit'. All we want is the opportunity to own or build our houses at a reasonable price. Yes, some of us were the 'something-for-nothing-generation' and expected the world to owe us a living (not me), simply because we do, but that was a long time ago, and many of those types of people were burnt in the financial crisis.

Does the government seriously expect us to submit to a lifetime of debt-slavery? It is our country, and our future. We can do what we want with it. The Brexit result has exposed the underlying issue of constitutional reform in this country. In the wake of the Brexit result, parliament started moaning about their so-called need and their 'right' to have a vote on Brexit themselves, presumably with the intention of scuppering the result right in front of our eyes. The underlying issue is that Parliament thinks that it is sovereign and not the people, and while it is written in what little we do have as a Constitution in this country, it is not really anything like a proper Constitution. What we really have in this country is a lot of parliamentary protocol, covering up with is basically a free-for-all.

We need to reform Land and Property, it is broken, we need to tax Land and Property again while freeing business to do business. Innovation and Production should not be taxed as they currently are. Unproductive gains on Property must be taxed, they contribute nothing to the economy and result in inequality of wealth. The wrong areas of the economy are being taxed. A vital part of making Britain work in a post-Brexit world is the right tax reform that does not punish Innovation and Production, but punishes Rent-

Capitalism. Reward Real-Capitalism, punish Rent-Capitalism. Reward Doers and Savers, punish Unhealthy Consumption.

THE EU

Given how the supply of building Land is so Rigged in our country, to the point that it infringes our basic human rights, if we had voted to stay in the EU, it may have been only a matter of time before somebody would have taken a case to the European Court of Human Rights regarding the UK Planning System and how it fundamentally infringes our right to settle where we want. And given how true this is, that our rights to settle are fundamentally infringed, it should be relatively straightforward to win the case. The plausible effect of a ruling against the UK planning system, letting someone build in the countryside, would have had the effect of causing a major change in the planning law, setting a precedent, and making the countryside available for building on again. The main pillar of the Planning Law, controlling and restricting the locations that can be built on, would be overturned on the sound basis of the human right to settle. I will talk more about legal action later on when discussing the options available to enact reform in the Planning Law.

I wonder if perhaps the biggest loss for our generation from leaving the EU may in fact be the loss of access to the EU housing market, and the affordable possibility to build your own home in these countries compared to the criminally high cost of basic Shelter in our country. Central and Eastern Europe are even cheaper, much cheaper. In Europe they let you build, so why not UK? It almost makes you wonder what the real reasons for leaving Europe were. I wonder if sometimes there are other reasons for leaving the EU. Were there Planning Directives in the pipeline that would have harmonised planning laws, and forced uk to let people build freely? If there was then this would be a huge development, that an ulterior motive for politicians wanting to leave the EU was because they didn't want brussels to force planning reform on them! But this is just an 'I wonder if'. I'm not seriously suggesting it was the reason, that is for somebody else to find out. It would make a huge number of people wish they hadn't voted to Leave.

THE CHANGING TIDE

We live in a society where the Shelter itself and the Land it sits on has had its Freedom of use eroded to create a Rigged Market of ever-higher prices, which forces us to place ourselves into debt-slavery for at least 25 years in order to buy very basic Shelter that isn't necessarily even freehold. In the name of what? I have shown how protecting the countryside is certainly not the real reason why we don't allow building in the countryside. It is impossible to justify the current Land and Planning Laws if the price is sky-high house prices. So in the absence of any moral or economic justification, the Market must Logically be Rigged to deliberately produce those ever-higher prices. That's just the excuse they use.

Over the past decade or so, the feeling about the Planning Law in our country has changed. It has changed from being broadly in favour of control and planning boundaries and conservation, to one of frustration and suspicion. Some of this change in perception has been due to my generation entering the sphere of public opinion as we have grown older, but just as much of it is due to the our parent's generation beginning to realise now that ever-rising house prices isn't all it's cracked up to be, if their children can't afford to buy the same sort of house they grew up in, regardless of how successful they are.

It is interesting and perhaps telling that the new prime minister Theresa May, while talking about Brexit and telling us that 'Brexit means Brexit' and moving to fix the long term immigration issue this country faces, has made virtually no comments whatsoever about the other huge domestic issue that Britain is facing, the Housing Crisis. Why is this? Does she intend to do nothing about it? Theresa May's constituency is in Maidenhead in Berkshire, near to the proposed Heathrow expansion. Heathrow expansion is now planned to go ahead, but she can still succumb to the pressure from her own constituents to push it elsewhere. I expect a reaction from the political establishment about housing reform will be along the lines of 'Well, we need to see the impact of Brexit and less immigration on the housing market first, and that will take a few years'. That will sound like just another excuse, along with all the other excuses over the years.

There seems to be something of a blame game going on at the moment on house prices between the Government and the Bank of England. It's now widely known that their relationship is not good. I suspect a big part of this is because of high prices, and both camps know that prices have become not just unsustainable, but dangerously destabilising. Both sides have done a huge amount to blow up the housing bubble to the greatest it has ever been. The government has mostly interfered with long term supply, and the Bank of England has stoked demand with 35 years of falling interest rates, and 7 years of Quantitative Easing. But they are all Guilty, because they are all the Establishment. They are the generational elite who knows they are onto a good thing, so they keep on passing laws and making policy to keep the status quo of ever-rising house prices.

Thus far, none of the political parties have come forward with any serious reforms of Land and Housing in this country. Even the minor political parties, UKIP and the Liberal Democrats, have not even touched this most major of issues that our country faces. I say that if any of them are serious about gaining long-term political traction in the wake of Brexit and lasting as political parties, then they need to start coming up with major attention-grabbing policies that actually solve the major problems this country currently has. It looks like we may be fixing the immigration issue that has been simmering for so long in people's minds. Now we must move on to the housing crisis. It is for UKIP or the Lib Dems to have the balls to come out and say that we must finally start to roll back the planning laws and in the name of fundamental Liberalism allow the people of this country to build their houses where they actually want to, whether it is in the countryside or in the middle of a city of halfway up a mountain. I say the names of these 2 parties because they seem to genuinely care about the British People, while the Conservatives and Labour are the establishment parties who intend to perpetuate (or should it be *perpetrate*?) the Criminal Status Quo.

I will be surprised if any politicians have the guts to bring real reform to Britain's housing market, so we will have to force it upon them, in the same way that Brexit is being forced upon them now. Except that housing reform is a genuinely popular movement. If the Establishment Elite cannot be trusted to carry through Brexit, as some of you would like, then how can they be trusted to carry out real reform of the housing market? They can't. They want to carry on Rigging it.

In fact, it wouldn't surprise me if we see sly new laws being introduced to further increase house prices while the government supposedly undertakes its housebuilding push. The government wants to permanently maintain house prices at these absurdly inflated levels, to enable their generation to cash in while they are alive. So they will look to pass further laws that will continue to artificially inflate prices.

Even so, the Bank of England and Government have to make a choice between keeping house prices on an ever-upward trend, or keeping the pound stable. We are now at a turning point in the economy and it is decision-time for the Establishment Elite.

If they choose to keep ever-rising house prices, then the Pound will collapse and inflation will get out of control, because the Bank of England will be in a dilemma and won't want to raise interest rates to bring inflation under control as it will stop house prices from going up. They have a choice to make that they will not be able to make, as they desperately want prices to keep rising. Parliament will never have the Will to bring real reform to the Land and property market, as it is in their own personal interests to keep prices rising, and real reform means that inflation-adjusted real house prices have to fall. If inflation is allowed to get out of control, then the cost of everything from milk and eggs to alcohol, televisions, computers and cars will skyrocket. This increase in the cost of living will at first happen with no wage rises to compensate, but not for long. Wages will start to rise, but that is only relevant if you are actually working. If, for example, you are a student or you are retired, or are reliant on benefits, you will see a permanent reduction in your standard of living. And high inflation always tends to bring high unemployment, so few people will be safe in their jobs if they are working. There is also a delay in wage rises occurring, so that prices of things rise long before wages does. So the price of keeping house prices on an ever-upward trend, as we have already seen in the 1970s, will be heavy. Pensioners' fixed retirement income will fall to a fraction of the current value relative to prices of goods and services, students will have to take out larger amounts of debt to fund their education.

If so, why, and what benefits are there of this for us, to so go against the trend of Liberalism in the 19th and 20th centuries? Why is truly so easy for ruthless people to make so much money out of property, pay no tax on it, while the rest of us 99% watch our living standards get eroded away over time?

How long can the government keep the status quo going for? Brexit already means it is cracking apart.

The only way this economic model in the UK can be sustained, of ever-rising nominal house prices, is if we allow dangerously high inflation in the rest of the economy to enable wages and prices to catch with house prices.

WHAT NEXT?

I am trying to show you that the Establishment Elite has Rigged the Housing Market, just like they have Rigged much of the rest of the economy and society, including theoretically unlimited immigration. It's even possible to say they have Rigged the divorce system to keep the 99% fighting each other so that we cannot progress. We have seen the start of the Rout of the Establishment Elite with Brexit and the American Election, and soon Europe. They are the vested interests in the system's status quoof elitism, cronyism, huge immigration to keep wages down, and ever-risinghouse prices. It's all part of the same overall system in the UK. But now it is changing. They cannot game the system towards higher and higher house prices forever. At some point the system has to break, and 2016 has seen the start of this as popular revolutions sweep the Western World.

To summarise, there is no easy way out of the current housing market process that will not be incredibly painful for some sections of society. If the house prices to wages ratio adjusts via falling house prices, then everybody who has bought into the market for the first time over the last 5-6 years is going to lose most of their equity or fall into negative equity. This will be highly deflationary for the economy and will cause it to crash. However, if the ratio adjusts via high inflation and also wage inflation, then pensioners will lose the purchasing power of their pensions, and interest rates will have to rise to match high wage inflation, which will make house prices stand still relative to wages or even fall too. There is no good way out of the current economic situation. It is impossible for the government to find a way out of this situation that enables people to have permanently high prices without enslaving an entire generation of people, which is just unacceptable.

Housing reform will likely create further political turmoil in this country.

Real inflation-adjusted house prices have to fall, and house prices relative to wages have to fall in order to solve the housing crisis. The vested interests cannot have it both ways forever. It is unsustainable.

It remains to be seen whether Theresa May and her Cabinet have the strength to force through real reform of the Land and Housing market. The signs thus far are mildly encouraging. After all, they are determined to force through Brexit when most of the rest of the political and economic elite are trying to undermine the decision to leave the EU. They must have great conviction to do this. And they have also made the recent decision to expand Heathrow airport in the face of some opposition, though not nearly as much as Brexit. But yet again, so little noise has been made about confronting the housing market. The longer they leave this, the more they look like just the same bunch of politicians who have no intention of truly reforming and freeing this vital market. I feel the greatest test of their resolve is whether they have the strength and courage to reform Land and property. This is ultimately as big an issue as Brexit, and is vital for the future of our country. This is our Freedom at stake here. It is about the survival of the people and this country.

If the young turn their backs on owning homes, on participating in society, and the wider way of life, as they have been showing signs of doing, then what future is there for this country? What if we decide to leave en masse for other countries because their homes are so much cheaper or they let you build?

Look, we spend our lives chasing ever-rising house prices, regardless of the size of house that we can afford or how wealthy we are. It affects all of us. This makes us economic serfs. It makes us Wage-Debt Serfs. It is not Left-Wing to say that. Would you like to be able to get around this by building your own Home, practically anywhere you wanted? Would you like to be able to buy your house for a lot cheaper that you currently can? Would you like house prices to stop going up or even fall relative to your wages so you can save up and then upsize? Well, you can. It will be entirely possible to achieve this. It is *not* some Unachievable Utopian Dream, unlike Socialism.

THE SELF BUILD AND CUSTOM HOUSEBUILDING ACT 2015 - A MOVE IN THE RIGHT DIRECTION

If there is one sign of change in the housing market, then it is this act. It was introduced in 2015 with the aim of assisting individuals and families in their dream of building themselves a house. It forces local authorities to maintain a register of people who want to build their own houses on a plot of Land.

The local authorities and councils absolutely hate this act. They hate it because they hate people building houses. They like having power over others in society, and it is mostly the only job satisfaction that they get. They like to have the power to say No.

The problem with this Act is that it doesn't actually let the people build their own homes. It just forces local authorities to keep a register of those who want to.

I have included the links below for your further reading:

http://www.legislation.gov.uk/ukpga/2015/17

http://services.parliament.uk/bills/2014-15/selfbuildandcustomhousebuilding.html

http://www.planningresource.co.uk/article/1339206/why-planners-concerned-new-self-build-duties-local-authorities

'MODULAR' (PREFABRICATED) HOUSING AND THE NEW HOUSING 'BOOM'

There is a new method of constructing houses that I want to draw your attention to. It's important that I do this, because the Government is showing great interest in using this new method of construction to solve the housing crisis. It is called Modular Housing. This is where most of the structure of the house is built in modules that can slot together, inside factories. The benefits of this method of housing are hugely reduced construction times.

But in the absence of any planning reform, all this speeded up construction time is going to do to the house building process is place more profit into the hands of the Land owner who selling his Land for development. And I suspect that this is one of the main reasons why the Tory Government is so keen on Modular housing. It speeds up house-building, so that builders can get more houses built and sold in a set time frame. This would usually mean more profit for the builder per year etc, but instead, because the supply of Land is fundamentally restricted and Rigged, you will see Landowners raising their selling prices for what building Land is available, to take much of that profit away from the builders. The benefits and profits of speeding up the building process will find their way into the pockets of the Landowners and existing house owners. It is all part of the great rigging process that conspires to keep raising the price of residential Land and property and making it unavailable to the public.

This is the same old way that has been done before to solve past housing shortages without doing anything long term. Again, that government is suddenly showing great interest in this new method of construction rather than relaxing planning laws, shows they have no intention of reforming the long term supply and demand issues, of reforming the Rigged market. Because they want to go on rigging it. They are seeking to protect the massive prices rises we have seen over the last 70 years.

Ordinarily, if a lot of new houses are built the extra supplythis creates will lead to downward pressure in prices as the law of supply anddemand exerts itself... but because the market is Rigged there will be nonatural downward pressure on prices, meaning we will be forced to buy intothese artificially high prices. Because the perception of these modular homeswill be that there are similar to the prefab houses we saw after WW2, their quality will be seen to be lower, and so the value may well decline over time rather than keeping up with more-traditionally built houses.

Tech may have advanced in 70 years, but these houses may still be seen as inferior to the brick houses built during the last 70 years too. And if we young people do buy these properties, we will still be mortgaged to the hilt, and most importantly for the older masses who managed to get into the housing market at the right time before prices rose too high, we will still not be able to buy their houses off them when they want to downsize or die. So it still doesn't solve the long term problem of the market being Rigged. And it creates a housing market within a housing market, where no-one has the money to purchase the older properties. So they will be left to go to rack and ruin by the obsolescence by newer and better houses.

People don't want to live in controlled 'modular' housing in cities, they want the Freedom and Liberty to live anywhere they want, in the countryside and towns and cities in their own country if necessary. Modular housing can play a part, if it is of good quality and can be used by the people to build their own homes where we want.

CHAPTER 6
THE OPTIONS FOR LAND AND PROPERTY REFORM

If Politics is partly about fixing the major issues in our country so that we are stronger as a people and can move our country forward, then the Housing Market and Land Law generally must be in the top 3 issues we face in our country. In fact I would say that it is the biggest domestic issue our country faces because it affects our future and has so effectively divided our society. And this is a major crisis that been brewing for 70 years. It has its roots in the immediate post-war era and has grown and grown since then to become the monster of issues for our society. And it is not only about our generation being able to afford a home, it involves older people, the poor, economics, our Way of Life, our Culture, and our Philosophy.

OPTION 1 - PARTIAL ABOLITION OF THE PLANNING LAW, FOR INDIVIDUALS AND FAMILIES, WITH GOVERNMENT SELLOFF OF LAND FOR THE PEOPLE

Or, in other words, *Letting the People of this Country Build their own Homes, Where They Want To.*

Liberalise the Planning system to let the people build their own houses, where they want. Free the people from living their lives trapped within Planning Boundaries and paying the criminally obscene Land Prices that have been allowed to manifest over the last 70 years. How can this be done without losing most of the countryside to houses over the long term? I have already argued that the countryside is not going to disappear just because you let the People build our own homes on it. You also achieve this by controlling your country's overall population growth. The most likely way to achieve this is by slowing immigration down to a trickle, which is now on the cards since the vote to leave the European Union.

The Planning Boundaries would no longer apply to people wishing to build a home that they are going to live in. It will still be difficult to build a home in certain areas such as National Parks, Military areas and areas deemed too inaccessible for habitation, but not impossible.

What is this? Essentially, the bulk of the Planning Law, the crux of it and the restrictions of where you can build, will not apply to individuals and families who want to build themselves a home. The People. This specifically and especially includes the location part of the law. That means that you would be allowed to build yourself a home practically anywhere in the country. Something which you are not allowed to do today, something which should be a fundamental right for every British person. The Housebuilding Corporations who buy entire fields and dump the artificial dense housing estates on them however, will have the same restrictions as before. Nothing will change for them, the Planning Boundaries are still there.

How would this work? What impact would it have on current house prices? This will vastly increase the amount of Land that is potentially available to build houses on. So this will increase supply of Land, and also of houses, putting an immediate stop to the depressing annual rises in house prices that we have grown used to. You would have to apply for planning permission, in the usual way, but because you are an individual or family and have fulfilled certain other criteria pertaining your characteristics and situation as people, most of the planning law will not apply to you. The home will still have to look reasonably nice and 'amenable', and most importantly it will still have to conform to all the building regulations and controls that make our homes safe. But in Principle, *you are allowed to build what you want, where you want it.*

So who will be allowed to do this? The British People, that is people who were born here and are British citizens, and maybe those who have settled here and been here for more than 2 decades. In arguing for this solution, I am essentially arguing that planning control and restriction should shift away from Location and onto the Person themselves. This is to ensure that not too many people are able to build their homes at any one time, and so that we do not get vast influxes of foreigners who think they can take over our countryside and build foreign cities in our Land. Restrictions still need to be applied in some form, because we are a small country, and cannot afford to act like the USA, Canada or Australia and encourage large numbers of foreigners to settle here in their droves. They have to have proven themselves that they are serious about staying here.

Because the politicians are Vested Interests and have not the will or the energy to undertake sufficient reform of Land and property in this country, I argue that instead it is much more straightforward and easier to just repeal most of the law surrounding planning that has been built up since 1945. It is a lot easier to partially repeal through modifying it by, say by letting the People build their own Homes where they want, than by carrying out hundreds of micro-economic tweaks that will be guaranteed to have unintended negative consequences.

For the naysayers who say that the housing system needs to be controlled by local and central government, on the basis that development will be haphazard and have a severe impact on infrastructure, I have a few things to say. Firstly, the vast majority of people will want to live not too far away from where they work. And as Work usually happens in towns and cities for most of us, that means building houses in and around existing towns and cities or not far outside in the countryside, say about 30 minutes drive at most. Will parts of the countryside disappear because you allow the people to build what they want where they want? No, because people will typically be sensible about where they choose to live. They will want to live near to work, near to major infrastructure such as motorways and railways. They will not want to live right next to main roads because of the noise pollution, so this means that ribbon development will no longer be an issue. Incidentally, I argue that the threat of ribbon development went largely obsolete when cars became widely owned. People will want to build their homes within 10 miles of a motorway and/or a railway, a major town, or city.

The Nimbys should have little reason to oppose this solution. Note that I am saying that only individuals and families should have this fundamental right, which is of benefit to Nimbys and Conservationists themselves as it means that they themselves will be able to create their own Home where they want. Big Developers will still be subject to the strict controls and planning process that is currently in law. There could also be limits on the amount of Land that each Landowner could sell off, to ensure that there is balance. This is so that the countryside is protected from the disproportionately huge housing estates that can pop up in a short space of time and the blocks of flats that can appear in the wrong parts of London.

Being guaranteed your own plot of Land, or at least the opportunity to buy one, provides a great life goal to work towards for those in the public sector who are not paid much. The Police, Army, Doctors and Nurses and Civil Servants, can all have affordable homes if the Government was to sell off some of it's huge amounts of Land below market value to young self-builders. The Government could use the money raised from these selloffs to fund the Infrastructure projects that this country needs, or at least to pay down the national debt. This is a great way of getting people to participate it our society, giving us something to aim for.

The current drive to build more homes just benefits the big house-building corporations and the lucky few Landowners, by allowing them to build more of the housing estates that so many people see as a blight on our society. This solution will negate that.

Rolling back the planning law will risk alienating some of the rural grassroots Conservative supporters. But I also argue that it is more likely that a majority of rural dwellers *want* their descendants to be able to live, build and own their own home in the countryside, for a reasonable price. And not just some tiny Hovel that is restricted by size, the bare minimum sized house possible; People want to live in houses that suit their lifestyles and dreams. And I believe they would understand and agree with the actions of the government in rolling back the planning laws.

Who would be against this option? The Establishment Elite, and the older Professional Classes. Why? Simply because this changes the status quo, frees people, and allows people to get around submitting themselves to a lifetime of debt-slavery by creating opportunity to make other more economic sacrifices. It means that the younger generation does not have to be forced to buy overvalued properties simply to enable the older generation to cash in on their gains in the Housing Market. Landowners up and down the country, on the other hand, should not be against this, as it enables most Landowners to sell off a portion of their Land to build a house or two, while they get to keep hold of the rest of their Land. Before, they could not do this as only Land very near to town boundaries stood any chance of being allowed to be built on. The Political party who correctly sees the Housing Question as a way to get the under-40s on-side for the rest of their lives, should be open-minded enough to adopt this option. The rest of the Political Parties may be vehemently against this. Remember, this option essentially brings to an end 70 years of Elitist control and frees the people to live where they want, for a lot less money. People will be able to truly do the job they want to do, not be forced to due to circumstances, if they are able to live where they want for less money and then give up the jobs they don't like doing. This is all about having the Freedom to live the life you want to lead: about living where you want to live for a reasonable price, which means that you can do the job you truly want to do in order to create the life you want for yourself. It's about National Happiness and National Liberalism.

The other European countries, especially Germany, have a national culture of building your own Home. They positively encourage their citizens to do it, it's part of the German dream come true, similar in some ways to the American dream. Contrast this with the state of self-building in the UK. It just does not happen on the scale that should be allowed, and where it does happen, it only happens in very tightly controlled ways on the edge of existing settlements and whether you get planning permission to build is really a game of luck and how the planners feel. Germany has a strong economy, with a similar population density as Britain, but unlike Britain they actually let you build your own house, practically anywhere. If you don't believe me, carry out your own research. You will see very quickly the opportunities that you have from the countries of Europe.

The Planning Laws should not apply to individuals and families who want to build their own homes. The people of this country should be Free and able to afford to build their own home almost anywhere in the country.

OPTION 2 - GOVERNMENT SELLOFF OF Land TO THE PEOPLE, WITH DEVELOPMENT RIGHTS ATTACHED, WITH THE INTRODUCTION OF PROPERTY CAPITAL GAINS TAX AT SOURCE AND AN ANNUAL Land TAX

This is a 2-part solution that combines elements of Options 1 and 3. The state, which owns more than 2million acres.

The Government starts a selloff of its Land-holdings, including the Land held within its Trusts, at a discount, with development rights attached, for the People to build their own Homes. It encourages the largest Landowners to do the same. It also abolishes Principal Private Residence Tax Relief above a certain profit made on the sale of a Home.

I argue that there should be a short-term selloff of government Land to enable us to build our own houses, and a capital tax introduced on the gains in property that people and companies, taxed at source. In the medium term, the planning laws need to be rolled back if we do not tear them up immediately. A short term Land selloff to the people of this country will be a fantastic revenue earner for the government too.

Accept that the uneconomic gains on housing are a transfer of wealth from the young to the old and need to be taxed, repeal Principal Private Residence relief and introduce a tax on the gain on sale of Land and property via the Land Registry, of at least 20%. I have argued how the tax-free gain on property and other assets via offshore trusts and companies have been a driving force behind the growing inequality of wealth in this country. I have shown how we, the 99%, have to pay exorbitant house prices to fund the tax-free profits of luxury housing developers as their high London prices reverberate out to the rest of the country's housing market, providing the direct mechanism of us paying debt off on mortgages to fund the growing inequality of wealth. We also take out mortgages to part-fund the trade deficit of this country, thus spending centuries of accumulated wealth out of the front door to other countries.

Remember that David Lloyd George brought in a tax on the profits of Land and Property values during a time when there were no planning laws at all i.e. when the Supply of Buildings was not Rigged at all and you could build a property practically anywhere you wanted. So if we now have a restricted supply creating abnormally high profits on Land and Property, what justifiable reason do we have for *not* re-introducing a gains tax on Land and Property? The inequality of wealth is just as bad as it was in the early 20th century. I would say that it is vital that we re-introduce the Capital Gains Tax on housing.

Abolishing or curtailing Principal Private Residence Relief has historically been seen as political suicide, that is, no party would ever want to do it because of the perception of unpopularity with the general public. But with recent political developments such as Brexit, and the movement against the status quo and the political and economic establishment elite, the climate appears to be changing. I personally, and most of the people in this country, can sense that there are great changes afoot for our society. I believe that the PM and her cabinet could get away with forcing this tax change through, and tax the gain on properties at source when they are disposed. This can be justified by showing that the rich are able to make tens of millions of pounds of tax-free gains on property, that has never been taxed. A flat tax of 20-40% paid at the point of sale by the seller on all property in the UK, regardless of the impact of inflation, would be a simple tax to administer, reinforced by the necessity to pay before the Land Registry recognises the transaction in law.

OPTION 3 - SOCIALISATION OF ALL HOUSING AND LAND

This is the most drastic of all the options, as it is essentially Communist in nature.

The State takes over all private housing property throughout the country. This could be justified because the cost of a basic right, housing, has now become so expensive and the market for it so broken, and because it is causing the country to move back towards serfdom. At least that is the justification for it that would be used by the proponents of this policy. The mechanism works like this. All private housing is appropriated, without compensation, by the government. the biggest misallocation of economicresource to unproductive means that the world has ever seen, and because itdoes so, real business and innovation and productivity is suffering because ofthe huge sucking noise coming from the housing market taking in all thecapital, to sustain the ever-rising prices. is so densely populated that... Thegovernment owns all housing. Owning a house doesn't matter anymore,because no-one owns a house anymore - it's all relative.

The private business sector however, is left alone, and is allowed to carry on operating as normal, so as to maintain and encourage innovation in our society. This is necessary to enable economic growth and improvements in quality of life to continue. Business taxes are lowered or abolished, as appears to now be the movement in the world. Business also benefits from the socialised housing because there is no longer a huge capital misallocation in our society, freeing up capital for investment in the private business sector, not the housing market. This accelerates long term economic growth and productivity improvements. The government is responsible for building the housing stock required for our country. And workers are able to freely move from town to town, following their employment, because the government ensures there is a surplus of housing with enough empty housing around the country to make allocating a new home easy. So you can start to see the benefits to business of adopting socialised housing. All we have to do is apply online for a house in X location, the government finds one and allocates one, and we can be moved and settled in within a few weeks, at maximum convenience to us and our employer.

People can still get rich if they want to. People can still be successful and benefit from the better quality of life that wealth can bring. It's just that they cannot use their money in the housing sector of the economy, so they are therefore logically forced to accumulate wealth in more moral sectors of the economy, where investment typically generates real economic growth. They can just use their money to rent a bigger and better house off of the government, rather than spend (misallocate) a huge amount of money *buying* a house. Which is better for them, because rents are kept low to allow them to benefit from this over the long term... So you can see how this housing system can benefit everybody, even the well-off, because at the moment every home is hugely expensive, and if you manage to make a lot of money in this world, you end up spending a huge portion of it just on a house.

So how does this work? The Government appropriates the entire housing stock of the country that it does not already own, without compensation. However the mortgages and debt on housing are also taken on by the government, including business debt. The people who lose the most are those who have the most equity in their houses, the rich. Precisely the same people who have not been paying any tax on the profit they make when they sell their property. And the people who gain the most from this are the people with negative equity or no equity but the monthly burden of high mortgage interest payments. This option has credibility in our country because of the immorality in Rigging the Housing Market. Everybody then pays a low nominal amount of rent to the government each month to enable them to live in houses they are already in. The government takes on the responsibility of major maintenance of each property, deciding whether to maintain or demolish and rebuild with something more modern. The government carries out a building boom to ensure there is an excess of property, to keep living space available for each town and city, and rents low.

Would you like to be able to not have to worry about paying a mortgage on the house you live in, and instead pay a nominal amount as rent each month, guaranteed to be low by the government, when you want? Would you like to be able to move freely and easily around the country, to follow work or your dream, to easily move to a different part of the country? Would you like to be free of Wage-Debt Serfdom? With Housing Socialisation this is possible. Owning property doesn't matter anymore, because no-one else in the country does. Think how much easier your life could be.

But when the young are turning their backs on home ownership, they are also partly turning their backs on the concept of private property, and that is when they become susceptible to the concept of housing socialisation and hard-leftist views. Even though the Tory Government has stated home-ownership as one of its main goals for our society, So their housing policy cannever be seen as credible.

DECISION-TIME; AND THE IMPACT OF REFORMS

I have given a number of different reform options and now it is time to make a decision.

Option 2 is the option that is halfway between Options 1 and 3. However it does not provide real reform, and the Land that Government owns is not spread widely enough across the whole country to meet the requirements of those who want to build their own homes. I do feel however, that the tax on property gains at source is a good idea that should be given serious consideration by any Government. It is obscene that people have made profits on sale of their main homes of more than £1million and ot paid any tax on it while there is a housing crisis.

Option 3 is the Socialist option. In fact, it is not just Socialist, but outright

Communist. And given the recent world history of Communism and the things that have been done in the name of it, it is not workable. As Socialism often does, it looks appealing to people for its Utopian vision. But in reality it will not work. The state will be incapable of fulfilling its obligations to produce and maintain the entire housing stock. It is incapable of doing that at the moment with the planning law and the council house stock let alone if the entire housing stock was nationalised. And you can see that localism has meant that houses are not built in Nimby-Tory constituencies. Leftism is a trap for young people to fall into. Again, it looks appealing on the outside, with its 'redistribution' and 'fairness', but it does not work.

Which leaves us with the first, Option 1 - Giving We the People the Freedom to Build our Homes outside the Planning Boundaries, paying a reasonable Land price, and not constrained by Rigged Land Prices and the Wage-Debt Serfdom it results in. This is the option that is the most reform-like in nature and which therefore be mostly likely to solve the long term problems, and it will clearly be the most popular with the People of our country.

Let's ask ourselves the question that is one of the roots of Nimbyism. Why should we let a Landowner coin it in to the tune of tens of millions of pounds when we ourselves are not allowed to build ourselves a house outside the Planning Boundaries? And other Landowners stand no chance of gaining from development due to the Planning system lottery? It's a justifiable concern, and that is what is happening with the status quo. And Option 1 resolves this concern.

What would happen to Land prices if we were to partially repeal the Planning Act? The result of the repeal would be to increase the quantity of Land that could be built on by a factor of around 500%, while at the same time still having restrictions in place for big housing estates. This takes into account the realistic prospect of the Land in national parks and other poor-quality terrain being unsuitable for development. This huge increase in the supply of development Land relative to demand would soon stop rising house prices in its tracks. But house prices should not crash. This is because there will initially only be a trickle of people who will immediately take advantage of the Freedom to Build, while Landowners, keen to cash in on their right to develop their Land, will rush to sell off sections of their Land. This will cause Building Land prices to fall dramatically, reducing the financial barriers for the People. The trickle of supply will then start to grow, as more and more people take advantage of the low building Land prices relative to the price of houses that have already been built. The result is that after a few years we will start to see many more houses being built, in locations that people actually want to live. And the House price to Wages ratio starts to come down.

This solution represents the best possible compromise between Nimbyism and the Freedom for We the People to Live or Build ourselves a Home Where We Want to. I wrote earlier that a root of Nimbyism was the justifiable concern about artificial and manufactured toy-town housing estates erupting out of the ground in a nearby field, while communities were not allowed to develop naturally and gradually. And natural development entails the people being allowed to build or commission their own houses. My solution allows the people to build what they want where they want, and allows communities to develop naturally. The reason this solution will work is because sections of the countryside will not disappear, due to the way that human social behaviour expresses itself when people are allowed to settle naturally through their own decision-making. People will spread out, to a certain extent. The countryside will also not become cluttered with houses and roads that need maintenance, because most people will generally choose to live near other people, not far from Towns and Cities.

The beauty of enabling a Free Market in housing, for and driven by the People, is that Houses will automatically tend to get built where they are most needed. This is because most people will never want to live too far away from where they work, facilities and larger population centres. It's Human Social Behaviour. There will be a limited amount of building in the deep countryside anyway as people will not want to live too far away from the main transport links such as Motorways, A-Roads and Railways.

The economic effect of the savings we could make by building our own houses is as follows. A house that costs less to build through lower Land prices and less builder's profit requires less money in mortgage payments each month. This means that there will be less money paying down mortgage debt and more money flowing into the rest of the economy each month for other purposes, be it spending, savings accounts to indirectly invest in other economic endeavours, etc. So clearly there is a major benefit to the economy by enabling people to save money by building their own houses. This would also be a disinflationary effect, which, given the high inflation world we should be expecting now that the pound is a depreciating currency, will enable lower interest rates relative to what will be required for a falling currency.

The tax on housing gains will be a large revenue earner for the Treasury. This will enable taxes to be reduced elsewhere in the economy, meaning that Innovation and Production can afford to have much lower taxes to act as an incentive to us all. But most importantly, it will remove uneconomic gains from the housing market, acting as a disincentive for people to speculate in prices.

There *could* be a risk of the Landowners in each area forming a cartel together nearby a town, to fix the prices of Land to maintain high developmental Land prices. This part of the reason why I suggest the Government and biggest private Landowners can easily thwart this by doing a sell-off of its own Land at low prices, forcing Landowners to accept not much more than the agricultural Land value for their Land.

If we relax our planning laws while we stay in the EU, then EU human rights law will easily enable virtually anyone to come into this country and build themselves a house on our Land. We will not be able to challenge the right of other EU citizens streaming into our country and building houses. This means that if we relax the planning laws, potentially tens of millions of people will be able to settle here, permanently changing the face and fabric of this country. This is the only justifiable reason why the Land property laws should not be reformed at present - while we are members of the EU. The EU has a fundamental open borders policy, and because of the high standard of social welfare in this country, and the perceived high quality of life, EU citizens will want to settle here in their millions in addition to those already here if we let them build houses as well.

It is not in our interest to reform and relax our Land and property law in this country while we have an open borders policy with the rest of the world. If we do this then we risk millions of people coming here to settle and build. And then our countryside really will risk being lost to rich foreigners. The Japanese are a developed rich country like us, and yet they have never had an open orders policy. What I am saying is, that there are other countries out there, who survive perfectly well in this world, without having an open borders policy, for the benefit of their citizens.

If we ever get around to writing a proper Constitution for our country, we should write our basic housing rights and the Freedom to Settle into the Constitution that this country has never had, so that they cannot be tampered with again. The Fundamental Freedom of each individual to build himself or herself a Shelter for their living, and to a good standard, for an affordable price.

THE SCEPTICS

I am sure that there will be some people reading this book who just rather not believe what I am saying and accept the truth. Most of these people will be from the older generation, the baby boomers. And so, in anticipation of their desire to belittle and counteract my arguments in order so that they can perpetuate the status quo, here is the part where I preempt and refute them!

If you are a Generation X-er, and you are sceptical about the arguments in this book, then I have to say that rising house prices have affected you too. The value of your house is double what it should be, but so is the value of the house that you could have upsized to if house prices were more affordable. And if you didn't want a larger house, you would have had a smaller mortgage which could have been paid off sooner.

If you are a Baby-Boomer, and you are sceptical about the arguments in this book, then I have to say that you are the generation that has benefited most from rising house prices. And therefore you are least capable of understanding and having empathy for my generation, of whom many of us are in fact your children. Because you were on the right side of the housing market while prices were still cheap, you are the people who are most obsessed with property prices. But by the way, you have still been paying much more for your house when you did have a mortgage, so you haven't got out of it really. You still could have bought or built a larger house if the Housing Market was not Rigged.

If you are one of my generation, the under-40s, who actually doesn't have a problem with the housing market being this way, then I suspect that you are probably Privileged in some way, or a Fool. Houses are worth about double what they should be, and so the only reason you would not care about it is if you are already very rich through Inheritance or Trustafarianism, are a die-hard Communist who has no interest in owning property, or are one of a handful of people our age in this country who has made millions of their own back. And even then you should still be concerned about the current situation. If you are not, then you probably shouldn't be reading this book, as you may well be a lost cause.

For the people out there who currently own a house. How does that make you feel? 25 long years, an unnecessarily high debt-serfdom. Now think how much worse that will be for my generation. Do you still think we should just accept the system for what it is?

'You want to destroy our beautifully green and pleasant Land forever', I hear you howl. No, I do not. I have said earlier on how relaxing the planning law and letting people build in the countryside is not going to make the countryside disappear. I have told you how the fact that most people would prefer to continue to live in and near towns and cities, near transport links, and this is all within the wider context that the countryside and it's pleasant views are mostly man-made anyway, and is in a constant state of long-term flux. Trying to stop that flux from happening just makes our society less adaptive to change and less able to adopt new economic and social innovations. It changes because we change it, and it changes naturally anyway. So people really need to get away from this ingrained view that the 'countryside' is 'natural' and most of it must be 'protected' at all costs. The countryside is not going to disappear just because you let us build homes in it. And even if some of it does, it was man-made anyway. The economic result is that housing is unaffordable because of these laws.

But, you say, if we build on the countryside, we will lose our food production capacity and therefore we will no longer be self-sufficient for food! I say that we haven't been self-sufficient for food for decades, and a large part of the inedible Rapeseed that we produce gets exported overseas anyway, to make oil. And that really does not earn us much money in the grand scheme of things. So we are using potential building Land to produce extensive low-value crops, which aren't even food.

Ah Ha, you say, but won't the traffic become unmanageable around towns and cities if people start to move outside of towns and have to drive in to get their shopping? Not really. In the 21st century, we are increasingly getting shopping delivered directly to our front doors which has less carbon footprint and impact on the environment than car use. Also, because there will not really be much extra traffic, the traffic will partly move from one place, the towns and cities, to more rural areas.

'Oh Well, It's a Free Market though isn't it?...' This is saying is laughable, because what we have is anything but a Free Market in housing. As I have shown you throughout this work, it is so obscenely Rigged it has resulted in us spending our lives trapped within artificial boundaries paying huge amounts of money for basic Shelter.

For those people whose parents say, 'Please don't read that book, it will just create bad feeling and won't solve anything', well that's what some of them are bound to say, and I have actually given ways for us to solve these problems towards the end!

To all those Nimbys who say "I've lived in this village for X number of years", I say: "Yes, but that is in the past, and this is about the future, and you are quite old, so you won't be around to see what it looks like, will you? It's our future and our country in the future, not yours. You've had your say, now give my generation theirs. Your nasty narrow-minded self-centred Rabid Nimbyism shows that you don't care about the younger generation."

Oh no, you say, but surely if you let people build anywhere they want in the countryside, then Land prices and therefore house prices will crash from all the extra supply? No, not necessarily, for a few reasons. Firstly, as soon as you do this, not everybody will suddenly decide to swoop down on the countryside to build themselves a house, it will happen gradually each year, many people will still decide to live in their existing house while they build, and it will a few years for this supply to come into the market. Yes, prices will stop rising for a very long time, and will fall in real terms and relative to wages but given that they are Criminally Disgusting already, that will be a *Good Thing*.

'Generation-Xers' and 'Baby Boomers', who are you going to sell your houses to when there is nobody from our 'Millennials' generation coming up behind you who is making any money? There is no chance that we will be able to afford to buy your houses off you. The Elite has been desperately trying to generate wage inflation since the Financial Crisis, but they have failed. The anti-immigration feeling in this country now means it won't be foreigners who will do it instead of us. And given we are all going to be mortgaged to the hilt after buying the new houses that the government wants to build, we won't be able to buy yours. Dwell on *that*.

CHAPTER 7
THE OPTIONS FOR OUR GENERATION

If Democracy is failing our generation, and we want to do something about it, then we have 2 options. We can fight for change and exercise our inalienable right to some kind of revolution; or we can leave the country. And if we leave, then this country will no longer exist. The Establishment Elite relies on us to do the grunt-work in the economy and they cannot operate this country full stop without us. None of our current Politicians have the stomach to carry out any of the real social and economic reforms this country needs. They are Weak, act only for their own generations, and have huge unresolvable conflicts of interest. So here I lay out these 2 options in more detail.

OPTION 1 - FIGHT FOR CHANGE; A WAY FORWARD, A MOVEMENT

We must come together and unite under a movement. We must create a real movement to force change in our society. This society clearly is not working for our generation, and so we must make it work for us.

The Establishment cannot just do the bare minimum, just enough, and hope it fixes the problem enough to keep us satisfied, while they go on just as they have done for the past 70 years. We have to create a movement that actually gets this done.

In the last chapter when I gave the options for Land and Housing reform, I also chose the option that was likely to be the most successful and popular with the country. The reform of letting We the People Build our own Homes practically anywhere we want, instead of the strictly controlled toy-town housing estates that periodically erupt in open fields enabling the lucky few Landowners and the Aristocracy to make tens of millions for each field they develop. So we have a common cause that can unite us as a
country.

But what do we do after we come together? How can we persuade our

Politicians to reform? There are a number of things we can do!

Surveys. We can start by conducting survey after survey for the population of this country, collecting the views on the housing market from the population of this country. It will become apparent quitequickly just how much support there is out there for Land and propertyreform.
Examples of question to ask include asking older people aboutwhether the would be able to afford to buy again for the first time now; How overvalued they think houses are; whether they like the big manufactured housing estates or would prefer to build their own house; what they think about building their own house in the countryside; whether they would like their children and grandchildren to build their own houses where they want.

In fact, for the expanded edition of this book, I plan to do just that. I and some partners in crime plan to carry out a number of surveys at various locations throughout the country, giving the people a chance to voice their views (i.e. Frustrations or outright Nimbyism) for the cause.

A National Housing March. (Or Many) I urge a multi-million-man march in London and the cities of this country. Millions of people, marching on London and other cities to demand real reform to the housing market. If we can succeed in bringing more than a million people together for a peaceful march in Westminster, in organising a mass demonstration by people from all sections of society, not just the young, then we can show the government that we truly mean business, and we just *will not stand* for the continued outright Rigging of the Housing Market. Why should we do this? If we try to apply pressure to parliament over this issue without taking some kind of action ourselves, they will just sit on it for years in the name of 'debating', deliberately stretching the process of reform out as far as possible. If we try to argue for a referendum, that will take years to achieve too. While I do agree with the concept of referendums, it will take too long unless we force the issue sooner. Whether or not the government decides this is a big enough issue to warrant a referendum i cannot tell. But unlike the EU, which we had a previous referendum on tojoin and leave, sort of, we have never had much of a say at all on the state ofthe housing market, so we can argue that the government should just go ahead and reform without a referendum. We've never had one before on housing, despite all the laws they have enacted to rig the market, so why have one now? Lets just force the issue on them. I have seen various newspaper articles about fixing the housing market over the years, and even more so this year, as the crisis comes to a head. But the kind of people who are writing these articles are not the kind of people who have really been affected by the crisis. They are mostly older, middle-aged people who got into the housing market at the right time years ago when prices were so much cheaper.

This Great National Housing March should be planned months up to 9 months in advance to encourage maximum participation in the millions. It should be advertised in newspapers and put on the news. The date should be etched in as many people's minds as possible. But it should not take place in only a few locations. Every town as well as every city should have its own demonstration, and all these demonstrations should take place on the same day. There should be placards ad posters stating 'Build Not Buy'!

Petitions. Create online petitions on the housing market. Create petitions for every constituent issue that is out there on the housing market, including all the issues in this book, and create a separate online government petition for each one. Create a petition for restricting or ending Principal Private Residence relief. And then explicitly target the under-40s over the rest of the population to get people to sign them. And then if enough people sign them, parliament will have to debate them. Don't let the other biggest issue of this country, the housing crisis, get sidelined and drowned out by Brexit over the next 2 years. Brexit is ticking along nicely in the background - don't let the media use it to distract us from the main issue that affects most of us on a daily basis.

Nimby-Neutralisation. We must attend the Planning meetings in our droves and make our cause known. We must outweigh, drown-out and drive out the Nimbys in a clear majority for reform and change. Make it clear to the Councils and Local Authorities that there are people out there who oppose and take a different view to the vocal Nimby-Tory Minority.

Settlement. What are they going to do, if we decide to suddenly pitch up in our thousands on the field of a willing Landowner, and start building houses? Are they going to send in the army from our own generation to get rid of us?

Form A New Political Party. A new or existing Party must take up the cause of Land and housing reform. Whether it is the Conservatives, UKIP or the Liberal Democrats, they must take the reigns and press forward with Land and Property reform. They must should compete with each other to offer the best and most liberal reform. Perhaps this is a chance for UKIP and the Liberals to regain support in the wake of Brexit. The recent good showing of the Liberals in the Witney by-election, David Cameron's old constituency, shows the potential they have to stage a major comeback.

We must drown out the naysayers, the vested interests and the Nimbys who will try and stop us. How is it for them to dictate house prices to the rest of society by rigging the market, when it's not even their future, and it won't matter for them because they are long-dead?

We can boycottnew-build houses, with their ever higher prices. This is a way of showingthat we will not be cowed into submitting to huge mortgages just to buy anew house, just to cement in place the criminally outrageous house prices thatthe older generations are desperate to cash in on and make permanent. I haveshown how the market for new houses is even more controlled by the bighousebuilders, taking advantage of the laws to their own advantage. Perhapswe could even boycott the housing market altogether. This is alreadyoccurring naturally because people can't afford to buy in the first place. Butlet's try and persuade those who do have the money to buy or move, not to doso. Now that more houses are being built, we should boycott the housingmarket, to cause maximum damage to Land and House prices at just the timewhen more supply is supposedly finally coming into the market. We canbring down the market, simply because they cannot force us to buy houses,can they? Vote with your wallets! We have the power, because we are thefuture of this country! It is perfectly reasonable for us to do this, because weare merely counteracting and cancelling out the Establishment Elite'sdeliberate Rigging and obsession with house prices. Take action, or rather,Take Action by doing Nothing!

Cheap Merchandise. T-Shirts. Caps. Mugs. Flags. Car Stickers. Even bloody jokes on Birthday Cards. Boats going down the River of this country with giant posters attached to them proclaiming how Rigged the whole Housing Market is.

Media Coverage. Where are the daily news columns dedicated to the housing crisis, written by the same reporters day in day out? Where is the running commentary on house prices and political and economic factors affecting house prices? Since the early 1990s we saw the continual stream of articles dedicated to Euro-Scepticism and leaving the EU. That happened for 25 years before we finally got the chance to vote on the EU again. The country has had to contend with sky high house prices for about 15 years now, but that doesn't mean we should have to wait another 10 years until we get some action from the government. We can force the change, starting now.

The Riggers and Nimbys and Conservationists may have gotten away with it so far, because they have been lucky that we have only been vocal to our parents and not in public. They have been lucky there has been no Movement yet. But soon there will be.

OPTION 2 - LEAVE

...And settle in another country where homes are more affordable and they let you build if you want to.

Things really are that bad for us. When Peter Hitchins says that the Young should leave the country and settle abroad, he has it half-way there. He is basically listing the 2nd option available to our generation.

My advice to you, my fellow under-40s, is to save up your money, and then leave this country to buy or build your home in a different Land. There are lots of interesting places where houses and the Land to build on are very affordable. Don't buy a house here, it is a Rigged Market and you will be submitting yourself to Wage-Debt Serfdom.

It is a Rigged Market. Leave this country and settle in a Land where they actually let you build a home and where homes are affordable. Take your savings with you before the Pound collapses while you still can, because when it really does collapse, you will have missed the chance. The collapsing Pound may trap any savings that you have, meaning you won't have much of an option but to stay.

The Establishment Elite have also been lucky that other countries such as Australia, New ZeaLand and Canada have not yet taken advantages of the situation facing the young of this country by inviting us over there to start a new life, and build a home for ourselves. They have not had a policy of attracting our young.

To these countries that spawned from Britain - *I invite you to start a deliberate policy of inviting us to settle in your country. To really show us the quality of life that can be had in your countries and the homes that can be bought there.*

I have Listed a few of the countries that you might like to take a look at and research.

And what's more, the advent of driverless car technology is just around the corner... long distances without any fatigue... enjoy touring... settle where you want.

IreLand. IreLand is still suffering from its housing crash during the financial crisis in 2007-2009. It also has a low population density at only 5 million people, compared to the UK's population of 65million on a Land area only about 3 times the size. So IreLand could easily take a population of 20million That's 15million extra people who could migrate there, millions from this country. It's also business-friendly owing to a low corporation tax rate of 12.5%. That means there will be plenty of job opportunities in the years to come, even if it is difficult to find work at the moment.

Sweden. This is a personal favourite of mine. Sweden has historically been a neutral country in any war, which makes it a safe option to settle in. It also has a low population density, with a population of 20million on a huge Landmass. This country could feasibly take a population of 100million people. Land is easy to come by and they let you build houses there too.

Australia and New ZeaLand. The classic place for British people to emigrate too, owing to its great weather, relaxed lifestyle and great quality of life. Low population, huge amounts of Land. Their house prices are on the high side, though not as high as ours, and it is much easier to get permission to build a home. I suppose it depends on if you mind the distance from Britain and your family.

Canada. Quite possibly the biggest English-speaking Landmass in the world. It is more than double the size of the USA, but only has a population of 35million people. This country has perhaps the best potential for you to build your own home, with a population large enough to make looking for a job straightforward. The houses are cheap too. It gets cold in the Winter, yes, by Global Warming means that it is warming up quite nicely, and the Summers are hot anyway.

Open your eyes! Look how bad it is here compared to everywhere else! Even when they are building houses, they are trying to get us to pay high prices for them, so that there is no way out of the debt trap for us. But there is a way out, physically. Leave the country! They cannot stop us from doing so, they can't keep us here, can they? And they cannot stop us from taking our money with us. But they might try to stop us.

As for the other countries, which countries have the cheapest house prices relative to earnings? Which countries let you build a home for yourself, or any size that you can afford? These are your financial yardsticks for gauging the attractiveness of these countries.

Organise. Or Leave.

CHAPTER 8
ONWARD

I say that it is now the time that a Liberal movement is started to free the housing market, so that all of us may be guaranteed a cheap, affordable way to own our own houses, so that we can live our lives the way we please, so long as we are willing to work for it. The current situation is a form of slavery for the young, so that a bunch of asset-rich, older Nimbys can continue receiving their generous state and private pensions off the back of our hard work.

Ask yourselves: Is this Freedom? Is this Liberty? Decide for yourself, but I *know* that it is not. And yet, we scarcely seem to have noticed this erosion of Freedom via the Housing Market. We live in a world of constant addictive distractions, from Smartphones and Computer Games to Television and the same old monocultural Coffee and Food shops on every street. How much of this is actually enjoyable? Is it there to keep us sedated and distracted from the underlying Truth about our society and way of life? We spend our lives trapped living inside artificially created Planning Boundaries, where we are forced to spend a large amount of our monthly wage to pay for basic Shelter. If we own our Hovel, we have had to pay through the nose for it; if we rent, it is dead money.

In Chapter 6 I chose the option to get away from this situation, that I believe was most suitable for Land and Housing Reform in our country. This was the Freedom for us to Build our own Homes where we want. It means we can escape the Planning Boundaries and the criminally high Land prices that we have to pay to own a Home.

Philosophically... This is also about giving us the Freedom to Settle, and the Freedom to Create. The Freedom to live our lives in the way that most of us dream about in some form of another. At the moment we do not have the Freedom to do this, and have not had so for 70 years. The current Land and Property Law infringes our Human Rights.

Economically... Allowing us to Settle where we want to will automatically ensure that houses are built where they are needed. Allowing us to Create will boost and stimulate the economy outright. The supply of houses will go up dramatically. The gross misallocation of economic resource into ever-rising house prices will end, freeing up capital to be invested into other parts of the economy, making it more dynamic and improving long-term economic growth.

Politically... The Party which pulls this off is going to be the saviour of the Housing Crisis. But what is the real prize of fixing the HousingMarket? The Vote of the young generation, the Millennials. And this meansthat the Party will have found a way to survive going forward, because at themoment the future of all political parties in the UK is uncertain.

Technologically... We have everything we need in our modern industrialised 21st century to achieve this. This is not the mid-19th century where you were constrained by transport and raw materials costs and access to civilisation. We have the Internet, Food Deliveries, Transport. We have the ability to generate our own electricity from green energy sources ourselves if we want to. We almost have Driverless Cars, which is really going to change our way of life, as transport tech has throughout history. The Countryside is so much more accessible today, and the towns and cities will be too, wherever you are.

Culturally... People don't want to be forced into living in towns and cities. They want a choice of where to live. The countryside is a hugely popular place to live these days, evidenced by all the people migrating out of London, and with the popularity of programmes such as Escape To The Country. So why is the countryside not more accessible? What did our ancestors fight for if we can't even afford a decent house or truly choose where we can live?

There is no point buying property in the UK currently. If you have the money to buy, it is much cheaper to buy in Europe and North America, and they let you build your own home in those places. My advice to we under-40s, is don't buy at the moment. Boycott the housing market. Save up, yes, but don't buy here. While older people will say that the UK property market has and always will go up, so there is no point buying anywhere in the world but in the UK, the fact is that at some point all this is going to go horribly wrong, either as a price crash, or will lead to inflation in the wider economy as it is starting to do, making the pound fall and devaluing UK property relative to the rest of the world. Or there will be some kind of revolution. It is an inevitable correction. The Riggers cannot have it their own way forever.

House prices need to fall by almost half before they are once again at a reasonable price. That's a 50% fall. Failing that, wages need to double from current levels to make current prices sustainable. And we are now at the stage where the people of this country are not too opposed to house prices falling by a substantial amount. If the Government does not abolish or roll back the planning laws in this country, then the Government must undertake a sale of its Land holdings at below market prices to enable individuals & families to build their own homes. This will benefit the government as well as the people by raising a huge amount of money that can be used to fund infrastructure projects that this country needs.

Look at what they are NOT doing... reforming the Supply side, relaxing planning laws, letting us build our homes! Don't look at what Parliament is actually doing with the housing market, look at what they are *not* doing.

Because the issue does not affect them personally, they are not really motivated to talk about it, or do anything concrete about it.

If Theresa May wants a *real* legacy, unlike Blair and Cameron, she should free the Housing Market. If she or Nigel Farage or Tim Farron areserious about getting the under-40s to vote for their Parties, then they will
recognise the political vote potential of carrying out this necessary reform. The real political and economic issue of the 21st century for our generation is not Brexit, it is the Housing Market. But I suspect that the
Conservative party is just incapable of making the reforms to our Land and Housing market, simply because they believe it will inevitably involve harming their core voters. And because they like the HousingMarket.

The basic human needs of Food and Clothing are cheap and easily obtainable for anyone, even the homeless nowadays. Sex is free too! (Sort of) So why not Housing, that basic Shelter to which we all have a right? Why is the cost of housing, which should arguably as cheap as the other basic human needs, be criminally expensive? It doesn't make any sense, does it? It is illogical, isn't it? There is no justifiable reason for Shelter to be so expensive compared to the other basic needs.

The real issue for us, our generation, is not 'Brexit' as it is put. It is the Housing Market. Brexit is almost a distraction, dare I say it. There has been media saturation about how the Brexit the result has divided us. But most people I have spoken to have accepted the result, whichever way they voted, if they voted at all. I suspect the Brexit debate is being played out by the media for as long as possible to act as a distraction from the real issues in our society. The media really has failed abjectly at homing in on the real issues in our society, or rather, it deliberately seeks to distract us and divert us from the real issues facing us.

If Brexit has taught us one thing, it is whether you voted in or out, it shows that the status quo can be changed and overturned, regardless of what the Establishment Elite wants. Our generation can change the current situation in the housing market and force the real Land and Property reform that this country needs.

After Brexit has been completed and net Immigration numbers have been brought down to the 'low-tens-of-thousands', as the government has stated is its aim, what is the next logical step? The next logical step is to reform the Land and Property law of this country. I have spoken earlier of the need to control immigration and population growth in our country, as reforming without controlling immigration will just give yet another reason for foreigners to come and settle in our Land. Once we have control of immigration, we can do this, we can safely reform Land and Property Law in this country.

I want the price that the older generations will have to pay for leaving the EU, to be the Liberation and Reform of the Housing Market.

This ridiculous concept where we are not allowed to build homes for ourselves on most of the physical Land in our country, despite it being fully liveable, weakens our society and makes it less adaptable to change. It does this because ever-rising property prices forces a vast misallocation of potential economic value and resources into an artificial store of value rather than being available for innovation, investment and strengthening our society. In the long-term context of civilisation, what long-term benefits does a Rigged Housing Market have? Seriously? None to speak of, and other countries don't have this policy of restriction only British-derived countries.

No serious patriot in our country can see that this system has any long-term value. What benefits are there from not making Land available for people to settle on, by restricting the Freedom of the tribe so fundamentally in where they can live? For the last several thousand years Europeans and humans in general were restricted in where they could live by the availability of Water... but now that these problems have been solved by 20th century advances, we should be allowed… and yet we are not! And there is no good reason for this! It's common sense to allow people to build where they want if the technology allows it and they are willing to make the sacrifices to do so, where before they were restricted by access to food and water.

We live in a society where we have had to accept unlimited immigration and where we are being forced to live in densely populated towns and cities. We are like Bees in Hives. Going out and working diligently every day for our rulers, our honey is being harvested for the benefit of the few, via mortgage payments, while we bees are forced to live in horrendously cramped living conditions. This is what it is like for our generation. The answer is not Socialism, as we have seen how that has failed, it is a revolution in the Freedom to settle and live where we choose, for a reasonable price. Away and free from the Hive that we are increasingly being forced to live our lives in. *Leave the Hive, find somewhere new to settle, and build your own Nest.*

If 1000 people decided to get together and buy some Land and divvy it up between themselves to build houses on, there isn't anything the government could do about it or enforce it's Rigged planning laws. What are they going to do, send in the army to stop people building Shelter for themselves on the so-called 'sacred soil of our green and pleasant Land'? That would cause an uproar!

This old, dated, broken economic model of ever-rising house-prices-relative-to-wages, caused by a Rigged Housing Market, perpetuated by a stuffy but hypocritical Elite will be swept aside.

Our generation does not agree with the current political and economic consensus of strictly controlled and limited housing development just to sustain ever-rising house prices, so that the Establishment and their generation can keep having things their way.

THE END

We, the young, and the ordinary people, the 99%, have been Pissed On from A Great Height. We have been derided, used, and trampled on by a contemptuous, arrogant and politically correct Establishment Elite. It was our ancestors who founded this country, whose Blood and Sweat and Tears in the Factories, Fields, and Battlefields made this country great… And what have we, their descendants, got for it? A system of extreme Wage-Debt

Serfdom, that if we can save up enough money to buy a house, *expects* us to *submit* to paying criminally high prices, just to sustain their *unsustainable* economic model of ever-rising house prices, which they have deliberately engineered over several decades.

The older generation are greedy. They expect to see ever-rising house prices and to keep their highly paid jobs until they are 65, even if that means that our generation never get the chance to progress our careers and move upward, and get some real money together. It is just *their* generation doing their best to protect their own positions at the expense of our generation. It seems that it is *they* who expect to have it both ways in life, without giving anything in return, it is *they* who are the 'something for nothing generation' rather than us.

The older generation and the Establishment Elite have mortgaged our future in order to keep their economy going, and *their* wealth rising. It has been a transfer of our future wealth to their current wealth. And that is why they will never reform the Housing Market. Because any reform must inevitably result in a transfer of wealth back to our generation. And they don't want to lose their relative wealth. And as they cannot be trusted to change this country for our benefit, we have little option but to force it ourselves, and I am wondering if we are now past the point when they can be relied upon to do it for us. So they should have little to no part in the future governments of this country.

The Corn Laws reform showed that our governments have a record of deliberately leaving reform off as long as possible, it is not just Europe that is slow at reform. We have been slow to reform too, just in different ways. We saw it before in the 19th century during the era of the Corn Law and the Famines it used to cause. We need to reform in different ways. We need Land Reform, and Land and Property Tax Reform. It is too easy to avoid and evade paying tax on Capital Gains on Property. There is a ban on building houses on at least 80% of the Land in this country. Do we need some kind of revolution to get real reform quickly?

We have every right to a revolution if we don't feel that things are going to change for our generation, or that we have to wait for certain generations to die of old age before we get to have our say and our way. We do not have to sit here and have that greedy generation tell us that we cannot change the status quo, because 'in Britain we do not have revolutions, that's not the way we do things here'. This country has never had a proper revolution. And the 2 countries famous for having revolutions, France and the USA, have broadly free housing markets where they let you build your own home for a reasonable price. These countries have no aristocracy as such, while in this country the aristocracy and government combined own 40-50% of all the physical Land!

We don't have to accept the current housing model for what it is, shrug our shoulders and go 'Oh Well...'

Why don't we just let people build and live in the countryside? What, really, is going to go wrong if we start doing that? Why shouldn't we? I have already invalidated the arguments against doing so, so we are left with no big reason not to.

What if the price of Brexit is other more fundamental change in other parts of our economy too? The older generation has got what they want with Brexit, but what's the price of that? We could get what we want with reform of the planning system. The older generation can't whinge and whine about De-Rigging the Housing Market if they got what they wanted with Brexit. They can't have it both ways. If they get something, we get something. And I think that something should be our Freedom to settle and build.

The Brexit vote has proven what can be achieved by the original British population of this country. We have managed to leave the EU, so we can also reform the Housing Market, and Land and property in thiscountry. So despite the political and economic elite desperately trying topush prices ever-higher, we can beat beat them down. After all, if Brexit canbe carried out successfully, mainly on the vote of the over 40s and over 60s, then surely the under 40s can achieve our own goal - Land Housing Reform.

But this requires us to be broadly United as a generation. And currently we are not United. Because, many of our generation have become supporters of Jeremy Corbyn's brand of left-wing Labour. I argue that Labour's Corbyn movement has just had the effect of dividing our generation by appealing to our leftist adherents and giving them something to support, and therefore keeping our generation weak and divided. This allows their generation to keep up from *organising*. We need to organise and get together under a common cause. It's the classic policy of 'divide and rule'. This actually works quite well for the Conservative party and suits them quite well that so many of our generation are supporting Corbyn, because it allows the Establishment to keep Rigging the Housing Market. Because it keeps our generation *divided*. And while we are divided, we cannot Unite together to force the issue of Land and Housing Reform, to bring down the Housing Market. The reality is that a party led by an old man is attracting young people to a cause that results in our generation being divided and weak. Think about it. It's a bit of a joke really. Reality Check: Old Man dividing Our Generation and keeping it from Uniting.

Jeremy Corbyn is an unwitting agent of the Establishment who is keeping our generation divided along the old lines of Left v Right. Until people ditch Corbynism and move towards supporting the main domestic issue that is undermining our society, we will not be able to come together and organise. Corbynism does nothing to solve the Housing Crisis. My solution to the Housing Crisis is not Left or Right. It is *Reform*, and *Liberalism for the British People*.

I have shown you that there IS a way we can make our voice heard. We just need to Organise together behind a common cause, a common issue. We have been ignored even though we are the future of this society, we must start to fight to make society work for us, rather than endure the opposite of taking the brunt every time the government decides to stave off the painful reforms this country needs, for the benefit of the older generations.

For those of you who didn't vote for Brexit and truly don't believe that it is the right direction for us to be going in, but respect the democratic process, now is your chance to get your own back on the people in our society who are responsible for it. And many of those people who voted for Brexit are also the ones who have benefitted from ever-rising house prices. After all, if the older generation can have their Brexit, we can have our Land and Housing Reform.

When it comes down to it, if a few million people decide to turn up in Westminster for a National Housing March and demand real reform and the Freedom to build, what can the government do about it? Are they just going to ignore us, and end up looking as bad, if not worse, than Tony Blair did, as this is a much bigger issue and a Domestic one, than the Iraq War? They cannot win either way, so if we decide to do it, we will win and force them into reform. It is inevitable. Which is why we must do it.

We are past the stage where the politicians will hope we will forget about it, if they make the right noises about appeasing us and then they hope they can brush it under the carpet at a later date. We have seen and learnt from Brexit how the government has been forced to push ahead with Brexit in light of accusations about a Westminster Stitch-up to backtrack on the vote to leave.

We are past the point of no-return in the Housing Market. The housing crisis has become so acute in our country, that an extreme solution is now the only logical way out of the housing crisis, if you look back at history. I argue that the housing crisis has become so extreme, in the manner of 19th century Russian Serfdom and Repression under the Tzars, that there is a risk that the solution will be an equally extremely one. Will it be the left-wing solution of Housing Socialisation? Will it be the Free Market view of rolling back most of the planning law to allow anybody, including companies, to build anything anywhere? Or will it be the National Liberalism view where individuals and families are allowed to build anywhere they like, in the name of fundamental liberalism for the British people, while big corporations are strictly controlled to ensure they don't dump housing estates in the wrong places? The Government's and Establishment Elite's preferred method of using the big housebuilders to build just enough houses in the same old strictly controlled way, so as to preserve ever-rising house prices, will not last.

The UK is clearly now going through a period of rapid change. Politics is in a state of flux, of which Brexit was a part, and Housing will be next. My generation will not stand for the imposition of serfdom on us by a greedy older generation of Politicians, Businessmen, Bankers and Nimbys. It is our future. We are not children to be spoken down to and screwed over.

I hope that 2017 will be the year that the Housing Market is exposedfor what it is, and the next major issue that our country faces alongside Brexitis brought to the fore. It is already fairly high up in people's minds as one of the top issues facing our country today. But I want the people of this country to learn that it has been completely Rigged in one direction for 70 years. I want to change people's perceptions of the housing market, to open their minds and to make them realise how we, the 99%, are being taken for the biggest ride this country has ever seen. Nigel Farage may well be right when he says that 2017 will be bigger politically than 2016 - *for additional reasons than he currently considers.*

The Land should be in the hands of those who can use it best. The Land is what we live on, eat from, and are clothed with. While Land may appear to be of less relevance in today's 21st century society with the advent of the internet and mobile telecommunications, it is still of vital importance because the price of the Land we live on has been Rigged.

Planning Law is one of the last vestiges of the Communist Era of Totalitarian State Control. Introduced by the Labour Government and reinforced by consecutive Conservative Governments it will be swept away, like Communism before it. There may be many minorities in society who will be against this change, be they Politicians concerned with the Globalist Status Quo, the Wealthy Elite, or Control-Hungry planning departments.

Is this an Evil Book, a Work Of Evil? Is it Mein Kampf or the Communist Manifesto? Hardly! All we want to do is free the housing market and let people build their own homes, we don't want to break things. We want to Create, not Destroy. I am not calling for some Bloody Revolution here, I am calling for a Movement. But we do have a inalienable Right to Revolution if successive governments are not willing to enact the change needed to fix our broken way of life. The Right is ours. Communism in Russia lasted for 70 years, from around 1920 to around 1990. The Housing Market in theUK has lasted for almost 70 years. It is now time for it to be swept away.Our society, but most of all our young, has nothing to lose and everything to gain.

Printed in Dunstable, United Kingdom

64918297R00068